Francis Harrison Pierpoint

Letter of Governor Peirpoint

To his Excellency the President and the honorable Congress of the United

States

Francis Harrison Pierpoint

Letter of Governor Peirpoint

To his Excellency the President and the honorable Congress of the United States

ISBN/EAN: 9783337234256

Printed in Europe, USA, Canada, Australia, Japan

Cover: Foto ©Suzi / pixelio.de

More available books at **www.hansebooks.com**

LETTER

OF

GOVERNOR PEIRPOINT,

TO HIS EXCELLENCY

THE PRESIDENT

AND THE

HONORABLE CONGRESS OF THE UNITED STATES,

ON THE SUBJECT OF

ABUSE OF MILITARY POWER IN THE COMMAND OF GENERAL BUTLER IN VIRGINIA AND NORTH CAROLINA.

WASHINGTON, D. C.:
McGILL & WITHEROW, PRINTERS AND STEREOTYPERS.
1864.

To His Excellency the President
and the Hon. Congress of the U. S.:

Gentlemen: It is a most painful necessity which has made it imperative on me to call your attention to the abuses of military power in Virginia. I have exhausted all the means known to me without success, to redress these wrongs. Your time is so much occupied that it isimpossible for me to go to you individually and relate the contents of the following pages. Having so many other duties to perform, to economize time I have adopted this method as most convenient to myself, with a desire also to consult your convenience, hoping that you may find a leisure hour to look into the subject here presented.

In addition to what is herein stated in regard to General Butler's department in Virginia, I assigned to myself the task of stating some facts in regard to the military administration of General Slough in this city of Alexandria during the last eighteen months; but as General Slough's case has has been referred to the Committee on the Conduct of the War, it may be considered premature for me to present the facts until that committee has had an opportunity to fully investigate the subject. I have only presented a few of the cases at Norfolk, and could only do so of those in Alexandria, without swelling this pamphlet to too large proportions. In Alexandria arbitrary power has taken a less range than at Norfolk, but in some of its exercise it has been more damaging to the principles of our organic law. What I mean by arbitrary exercise of power, *is a capricious exercise of power outside of the rules of war* in a manner to justly render the military authority obnoxious to the friends of the Government and the Union cause.

With a most ardent desire for the welfare and safety of our common country, and the discharge of a most solemn duty I owe to those whom I represent, I submit this subject to your enlightened and patriotic consideration.

F. H. PEIRPOINT.

ALEXANDRIA, VA.,
April 18, 1864.

LETTER.

On the 13th day of April, 1861, the Virginia convention went into secret session. Hon. W. T. Willey, now United States Senator, wrote to his friends at Morgantown to prepare for war—the State would secede. They must look for the worst. On the 22d of the same month a mass meeting was held at that place; that being court day, it was expected that speakers on both sides would be present, to address the people. A delegation of four hundred Union men came from the east end of the county. Before they came into town they halted, and passed a resolution with General Jackson's oath, that no secessionist should speak in town that day. They kept their oath. At one o'clock, with drum and fife, and national flags carried by different delegations, flags displayed from almost every house, ladies and children welcoming, the procession was formed, which paraded the streets for an hour. A stand in the public square was erected, the masses gathered around, appropriate resolutions were adopted, two speeches were made denouncing secession and the conspirators. The crowd refused to disperse, and called one of the speakers back to the stand. Several old soldiers of 1812 were there. One of them in great earnestness, said: "You must tell us what to do." "Do!" said the speaker. "Don't in your wrath kill any of these secessionists, who, like spaniels, are slinking around town. They want to be martyrs in a small way, to make capital for their cause, and get an opportunity to punish you, or incarcerate you in a dungeon. We can't spare you in that way. Go home, call your children around you. If any are married, call them and your grand-children. Tell them that with your strong arms, you and they have cleared out your farms, built your houses, and filled them with the conveniences of life. Point them to your barns and your stock; say to them that this is the product of the hard earnings of white men who never owned a slave; that now the slaveholders of the east, with the traitors in the west, are seeking to appropriate it all for the greater security, as they say, of their slaves. Say to your children, no; their object is to enslave the laboring white man, and to use your strong arms and all our substance to accomplish their wicked purpose. Then tell them to get their guns in order, and then in reunion let all, meekly kneeling around the family altar, promise before God to stand by the flag and Constitution of our fathers, and to defend it as long as life lasts. Then ask God, for the sake of his Son, to seal your covenant in heaven, and give you grace and courage to defend your section and country from the prey of the negro-ocracy of the south. That's what DO."

Upon this charge being received, the teeth of old men and young men chattered with rage, and they shouted, "we will DO IT."

In this spirit similar advice was given all over Northwestern Virginia. The people rallied, a great meeting was called by both parties at Fairmont, the center of secessionists, on the first Monday in May. Both parties were there in their strength; both flags were flying; fist fights commenced before nine o'clock. By two, both parties had speakers on the stand; secesh in the court house, Union out of doors. Before four, the secesh attempted to break up the Union crowd, and the Union men whipped them in a fair fist fight of not less than eighty on a side. This broke the spirit of secession in West Virginia.

The first Wheeling convention was called under the auspices of the Hon. John S. Carlisle. The second was called, the State government reorganized and recognized by the Government of the United States as the government of Virginia, I think wisely and rightly. The restored government put upward of eighteen thousand Union soldiers into the field during the first two years of the war. West Virginia has put in some three thousand since, in addition to which, a large number of the old troops have re-enlisted. These troops were as brave and as true as any who ever drew a trigger. The bones of many of them are now bleaching on almost every battle field, from the Peninsula to Vicksburg.

The State was divided by the consent of the Legislature and Congress. The officers and people indorsed the President's proclamation of emancipation, the policy of enlisting negroes in the Army, and the currency and the five-twenties. While West Virginia has put the troops above named into the field, her people have subscribed for a greater amount of the five-twenty loan than the State of Rhode Island, though one fourth of the territory is yet overrun by guerrillas; and Norfolk has established a national bank, with a capital of $100,000, and the amount all paid in.

After the division of the State, I consented to be elected Governor of the State, with the distinct understanding that I would govern it as a free State. The General Assembly was called together; it passed a bill providing for a constitutional convention; the members of the convention were elected by the people. The convention met on the 13th of February, 1864, in the city of Alexandria, and on the 10th day of March, with but one dissenting voice, adopt ed an amendment to the constitution abolishing slavery and involuntary servitude in the State forever.

The mode of organization of the State is complete, and as soon as the rebels are driven out, I expect to organize every county with loyal officers, under the old flag and a free constitution, without one cent of charge to the Federal Government.

I had the honor of acting as Governor of Virginia for two years, with the seat of government at the city of Wheeling. Troops were assembled there, mustered into the service of the United States, and sent to the field. Troops from other States passed through the city. The police regulations were, I think, about as good as they are in Norfolk and Alexandria. I had a small military force of two companies, with Major Darr for commander of the post and provost marshal. The military patroled the city, and when disorderly soldiers were found, they were arrested and sent to the guard house. When disorderly citizens were found, they were arrested and handed over to the civil authority. When soldiers were passing through or stopping in the city, the places where liquor was sold were ordered to be closed. When the exigency passed the prohibition was removed. I had intercourse constantly with General McClellan, while he was there; with General Rosecrans, who succeeded him; then with General Fremont; then General Schenck, and General Cox, General Scammon, and all the time with General Kelley. This intercourse was of the kindest nature, always on their part showing every disposition to assist in building up the civil government, and establishing the authority of law. A question was started as to where the military authority stopped and the civil began. The first case that occurred was the shooting of one soldier by another, at Parkersburg. The case was referred to me. I answered, the military could try by court-martial, or the offender could be handed over to the civil court. The latter course was adopted. The jury did not hang him, but awarded him ten years in the penitentiary. He is now expiating his crime. All similar cases took the same direction. Harmony has always existed between the civil and military authorities in West Virginia. The result is a prosperous people, where they are safe, and the great majority truly loyal, feeling that the government is a blessing.

I make these prefatory remarks to you, gentlemen, merely to impress upon your mind the fact that I am not a late adventurer in this rebellion, and a stranger to civil and military rule working together; but to remind you that I have been right in the midst of the rebellion since the commencement, and know of what I am writing, thereby hoping to call your serious consideration to the condition of things on the Potomac, Chesapeake, and Albemarle Sound. I now promise you that the information I give you, I do not expect to be pleasant, but it is no less true and painful to me. I do it in the discharge of high official duty, believing that you do not understand the extent to which military power is abused.

In connection with the movement in Western Virginia, I desire to make a single remark. In the border counties of Pennsylvania and Ohio, now represented by the Hon. Messrs. Dawson, Lazeer, White, and Morris, there was and still is a powerful secession element, ready to join the army of Jeff. Davis had they an opportunity. In the fall of 1862, they gloried in wearing butternut breast-pins, and at their public meetings indulged in the refined exercise of lapping out their tongues in imitation of copper snakes. So bitter were they in their denunciation of the movement of the restored government of Virginia, both in Pennsylvania and Ohio, that I gave orders if certain leaders came into Virginia to arrest them and send them out of the State, as not safe to circulate there. If Western Virginia had gone into the rebellion with spirit, she would have involved the whole border of western Pennsylvania and southern Ohio, and God only knows what the result would have been. The masses of a great and time-honored party had been taugh by their leaders that pro-slavery, secession, and democracy, were all the same, and the highest duty they owed their country was to oppose Abraham Lincoln, abolition, and the

Union. But fortunately for the country, many patriotic democrats came forward with a large number of the rank and file, and declared to the world that democracy, as they understood it, had a far different meaning, and have demonstrated the sincerity of their pretensions on many a hard fought battle-field, and are now shoulder to shoulder with the sincere Union men of all parties. Future generations will admire them for their courage in recognizing country before party.

By the act of the General Assembly, I was authorized to establish the seat of government in the bounds of the old State when West Virginia was organized. I fixed it at Alexandria. The county and municipal laws of Norfolk and Portsmouth and Norfolk county were put into operation about the 1st of June, 1863, by the election and qualification of proper officers, under the restored government of Virginia. Each officer, before entering on his duty, was sworn to support the Constitution of the United States as the supreme law of the land, and the laws of the restored government of Virginia—anything in the ordinance of the convention which assembled at Richmond on the 13th of February, 1851, to the contrary, notwithstanding. Lawyers, doctors, merchants, and every person doing business under a license, and clerks in stores, were required to take the same oath. Accomac and Northampton, Alexandria and Fairfax had been organized before that time. General Dix, with General Viele, commanded at Norfolk. I saw but little of them. General Foster succeeded. I found him to be a soldier, every inch, and after we got acquainted, were strong friends, as far as I know. General Naglee I pass over. General Lockwood commanded in Accomac and Northampton. I found him as true as steel, working faithfully to restore law and order, ready on all occasions to do his duty in assisting the civil government to establish its ascendancy, for which I commend him. In November, General Butler was appointed to the command of the eastern district of Virginia and North Carolina. I sighed when I heard it—I remembered New Orleans. There was short rejoicing at Norfolk among the ultra Union men; but in a short time the wail of woe came up. I was satisfied he was going to abrogate civil government if he could; that Unionism availed nothing if it lay between him and his object. That he was the seventh vial poured out to try the faith of the saints.

I visited Norfolk about the last of December, and fully

realized my apprehensions. Among the first orders General Butler issued, when he went to Norfolk in November last, was one threatening punishment to any person who used any disrespectful language to any officer or soldier in the Union army. Next was an order directing all permits granted by his predecessors to be returned to him. Then came an order charging one per cent. on all goods shipped into his military district, to go to the support of the *provost marshal's fund.* All vessels clearing from his district pay from five to fifteen dollars according to size, to the same fund. Oyster men were taxed from fifty cents to one dollar per month for the privilege of taking oysters; if in one field, fifty cents, if in two, one dollar. The provost marshal's court was fully established, trying causes in controversy, from one dollar to writs of ejectment; judgments rendered in land cases, and writs of possession given in five and ten days from date of judgment. One man, unable to pay a large judgment rendered against him, was placed in a felon's cell in jail and a guard put over his house. Costs, on about the scale of a civil suit in court, with a percentage for collection were charged, bringing money into the *provost marshal's fund* in a stream. Rebels, whom he had forced to take the oath to support tho Constitution of the United States, but who would not take the oath to support the restored government of Virginia, would go to this provost court to have their judgments against their neighbors, and for the further reason that they paid no internal revenue if they went to the provost court. But if they went to the civil court before bringing their suit they had to take an oath to support the restored government of Virginia and pay for an internal revenue stamp, which went into the United States treasury. The provost court saved all this, which was distasteful to rebels. This same provost court was issuing prohibitions forbidding tax collectors to sell rebel property levied on for State and city taxes. While I was there the provost marshal turned two men out of jail who had been committed by a justice for a misdemeanor or a felony, and were awaiting their trial before a court of competent criminal jurisdiction.

I left Norfolk about the 30th of December, sick, mentally and physically, and came to this city; some time afterwards I wrote General Butler a letter, calling his attention particularly to the abuses above alluded to, asking his co-operation in establishing the civil government, stating the opposition of the secessionists, and their desire to break up the civil rule. I also called his attention to military interferences with the city regulations of the markets, and reminded him that his provost court could make no sale of real or personal estate on its judgments and executions that would pass any title to the property sold. That a provost marshal's court was not the kind of a court contemplated in the Constitution of the United States in which a party could be deprived of his property by due course of law.

The General replied to my letter, expressing a desire to sustain the civil government; and in regard to his provost court, said "that no debts shall be collected save against those who are in rebellion against the United States in favor of loyal citizens, and when the property might escape from the *honest* creditor by reason of *confiscation*." In regard to the civil laws, he remarked: "The difficulty I find is that there are all the civil officers there known to the law, and none of the Government." He further said, "in regard to the stalls in the market, I have only directed an interference to prevent a collection by the city government of a year's rent in advance, which would virtually close the market and stop supplies to my troops."

As I shall hereafter refer to this provost court and the markets, I shall not comment further on these extracts here. In regard to the officers of the civil government, without the government, it is easy to be seen that the best men in the world would be discouraged in the execution of the civil laws when there was a provost marshal in the city releasing criminals, forbidding sales, assuming concurrent jurisdiction in everything, and threatening to imprison the civil officers; and as to securing debts of honest creditors against debtors in rebellion, I informed the General that there was the Court of Hustings of the two cities, the Circuit Court, and the District Court of the United States, all open with full jurisdiction in all cases, and by the laws of the State any person in rebellion was a non-resident for purposes of attachment, and that the attachment was a lien on real estate from the date of issue, so there could have been no reason for his provost court.

The next thing I heard was that Tazwel Taylor, of the city of Norfolk, was summoned to the council of the General to consult about the civil affairs of Norfolk. The Mayor was summoned also. When the Mayor went, who is a true and loyal man, he found, to his surprise, Tazwel in the room with the General. The General indecently catechized the Mayor for about one hour on the affairs of the civil government of the city in the presence of Tazwel Taylor, and through his promptings, much to the chagrin of the Mayor. Tazwel Taylor was the worst rebel in Norfolk, the agent for taking the confederate loan there; took $15,000 of it himself, and bullied others to take, until he raised about $75,000; was an aid on Magruder's staff while the rebels occupied Norfolk, and the most offensive rebel in the city to Union men, because he was the chief adviser of the rebels. Now, he becomes General Butler's adviser as to the restored government in the city. This may seem strange when you take General Butler's ultra views into consideration, but it is true. The General's letter was dated 10th of January, and his provost court is still in operation. The last civil case I heard of was the trial of a *habeas corpus* case, determining the custody of two children between husband and wife.

But to show the hollow pretense of taking care of Union men's rights: Harrington and Boyle, loyal merchants of Baltimore, brought suit and obtained judgment, in the Circuit Court of Norfolk city, against a rebel in arms against the United States. He had real estate in Norfolk city, and there was an order of sale, under an attachment duly issued. The order of sale, was directed to the city sergeant; and that those of you who are lawyers may see how easily a provost marshal issues a writ of prohibition, I will here insert the writ in full:

NORFOLK, VA., *March* 1, 1863.

SIR: You will not sell at auction the house and lot on corner of Cumberland and Wolf streets, belonging to James Campbell, and now occupied by Wm. Barrett, on Tuesday, the 3d of March, at 12 o'clock, to satisfy an execution in your hands, as you have advertised to do for a few days past.

By order of

LIEUT. COL. WHELDON,
Provost Marshal.
GEORGE P. EGAN, *Capt. & A. D. C.*
Deputy Provost Marshal.

To W. R. JONES, *Sergeant,*
Corporation Court, Norfolk, Virginia.

On the third of March he issued another in the same case, commanding him to respect the order of the 1st. Can there be a more flagrant usurpation of power than this? The man Barratt, who was living on the property, was a rebel; the owner was in rebellion, and this is the court that is to secure protection to loyal men of the North, lest the Government of the United States should cheat them out of their just debts. And this is only a sample of others. Immediately on the issuing of this order, Judge Sneed, of the Circuit Court, wrote a letter to General Butler protesting against interference with the processes and orders of his court. On the 23d of this month Judge Sneed had no reply; so this is the act and order of General Butler. This provost court takes cognizance of all cases of drunkenness, or other violation of city ordinances, has the party arrested, brought to his court, fines inflicted and paid into the *provost marshal's fund.*

I was informed in December that the sale of liquor by importers into Norfolk was going to be made a monopoly, and only a few were going to be allowed to sell. I heard more, but it was so incredible and discreditable that I could not believe it. I propose now to give you a few cases, though incredible as they may appear, truth requires their publication.

DANIELS & ZANTZINGER'S CASE.

This firm was one of the largest in Norfolk engaged in selling groceries and liquors and wood. About the first of January an officer called at their store and asked them how much liquor they had in the *store.* They replied about fifteen barrels. He examined the loft and cellar and found their statement correct. He then asked them how much they had in the shed. They told him he could go and see, and directed their clerk to go and show it to him. He went and found thirty-eight barrels there. He reported. They were immediately summoned before the provost court on a charge of fraudulently concealing from the officers of the United States the amount of whisky on hand; and it was mentioned in the charge, by way of recital, that the whisky was passed into the department, and being fraudulently retained, to the prejudice of good order and military discipline in the department. I here give the charge and evidence before the provost court.

UNITED STATES vs. ZANTZINGER & DANIELS. } *In the Provost Court.*

Charge.

Fraudulently concealing from the officer of the United States Government an amount of whisky consisting of fifty-three barrels, being an amount over and above the invoice given, upon due demand, to the lieutenant of the provost guard of the city of Norfolk. The said whisky being fraudulently passed into the department, and being fraudulently retained to the prejudice of good order and military discipline in the department. This at Norfolk, on or about the 1st of January, 1864.

Testimony.

Lieutenant Wood being duly sworn, says: About the 1st of January last I was commanding provost guard; was ordered to go and get an inventory of the liquor of Messrs. Zantzinger & Co.; asked them for a list of liquors on hand, and they gave me the one now in court. There are some fourteen or fifteen barrels of liquor on that list which were in the store. I asked Mr. Daniels if there was any liquor in that shed which was on the premises near the house; he told me I might go in and look for myself; went in with one of their clerks and examined; found fifty-three barrels of whisky, and other barrels of pork, fish, &c.; the whisky was covered over with hay and loose hay; Daniels told me he did not intend I should find any whisky, as he did not want any one to know that they had such a large supply on hand; if it was known they had so much on hand they could not get their price for it; also, said the whisky had been moved from the store house and put into the shed because the foundation of the store was weak and liable to give away under so great a pressure in the second story, where the whisky was; he said it was covered over with hay because the negroes were about there constantly at work, and they wished to conceal it from them; this shed seemed to be a place where hay, barrels of pork, fish, and many other things were kept.

Sergeant Holcombe, being duly sworn, says: Was one of

the provost guard on or about the 1st day of January last past; searched the shed on the premises near the store of Zantzinger & Daniels for whisky; found a large number of barrels of whisky in the shed covered over with loose hay and hay in bales; it seemed to be a place where hay, barrels of whisky, pork, and fish, and many other articles were kept.

George P. Kneller, being duly sworn for the defense, says: I have lived in Norfolk many years; am a State officer, inspector of provisions; have been acquainted with the business of Zantzinger & Co. for a number of years; they have always been large dealers in liquors, groceries, lumber, &c.; they had a very large supply of liquor at the time the rebels were here, and about the time they left; I know they had several hundred barrels of whisky on their premises; a short time before General Viele left this department I saw four four-horse Government wagons haul two loads each of barrels of whisky from the custom house to their store, protected by a Government guard; this liquor was some that was confiscated and purchased of the Government by Zantzinger & Daniels.

William Knight, being duly sworn for the defense, says: for a little more than than six months last past I have been a clerk for Zantzinger & Co. When I came there they had a large quantity of whisky on hand. They have received no whisky from any source since I have been living with them. If they had received any since I have been with them I should certainly have known it, as I am cognizant of all their business matters. I have not been employed there except in the day time; my duties have not kept me there at night, but I know that all the liquor on their premises was there when I came there to act as clerk. They built the shed to relieve the foundation of the store of too much weight, and put the whisky in the shed with other goods, as soon as it was finished.

Frank Smith, being duly sworn for the defense, says: I have been in the employ of Messrs. Zantzinger & Co., as night watchman, for nearly a year last past; I was employed in that capacity on the 18th of February last, and have been so engaged ever since; my habit has been to go on duty when they close business for the day, and to stay all night; I am not there during the day; my instructions from Mr. Zantzinger were not to allow any one to land liquor at their wharf while I was there on duty; no article of any kind ever came to their premises at night while I acted as watchman—liquor or anything else, except upon one occasion. One night some sailors from a schooner lying in the stream, came ashore there with a lot of whisky, as they said, in bottles. They got ashore there before I saw them, and were passing through the yard towards Wide Water street, when I hailed them; they begged me to let them pass through. I told them to get away from the store as soon as possible, which they did; neither Zantzinger or Daniels knew anything of the matter; Zantzinger told me if I allowed any one to land liquor there he would shoot me. They paid me forty-five dollars per month which I was anxious to receive for the support of my family, and I obeyed their instructions very strictly so as to keep my place.

Lieutenant Sewall, being duly sworn, says: I am in the revenue service. My duty for a long time has been to examine vessels and cargoes bound to Norfolk. I have been very strict and as active as possible in searching vessels for contraband goods. I have suspected vessels consigned to Zantzinger & Co., with having contraband goods concealed on board, but upon diligent search and inquiry have always found myself mistaken. Some ten months ago, Mr. Daniels remarked to me, in speaking upon the subject of smuggling whisky, they had no motive for being engaged in such practices, inasmuch as they had more whisky then on hand than they could dispose of. At his request, I went up stairs to look at what they had. I saw a very large quantity, in barrels, marked "cider vinegar," at least those I saw were so marked. I think at the lowest calculation, there was one hundred barrels, and I should not be surprised if what Mr. Daniels stated at the time was correct, they had three hundren barrels then on hand. I have examined the barrels of whisky found in Zantzinger & Co's shed covered with hay. It is my deliberate opinion, founded upon strict inquiry, that the whisky found there is no part of that brought to Norfolk by the brigantine "Judge Hathaway," concealed under the coal, supposing the "Judge Hathaway" did actually bring any to Norfolk. I felt quite certain at one time that the brigantine had brought smuggled liquor to Norfolk, and that Zantzinger & Co. received it; but I have had reasons to change my mind on that subject. Col. Whelden, the provost marshal, aided me in making inquiries into the matter, and we both came to the conclusion that Zantzinger & Daniels were not implicated in the matter of any liquor brought in the "Judge Hathaway," if any was brought, which seems doubtful. I want it understood, that in all the action I have taken in this investigation, my feelings have been enlisted in behalf of the Government, by whom I am employed, and that I have not been and am not influenced in the least by any friendship for Zantzinger & Co. On the other hand, I have not sought to injure them any more than my duty might require me to do so.

W. W. Wing, being duly sworn, says: I am the postmaster at Norfolk. Have known Zantzinger & Daniels many years. Some two or three months ago, the time not very certain, I was at their store. Daniels remarked to me that he had been very busy all the morning removing whisky from up stairs. He said that it was too heavy to be on the second floor, which was weak, and he had removed it to the shed. I saw them moving quite a number of barrels into the shed. I told Daniels that some one would steal all the whisky out of the shed, as all that was necessary was to take off a few boards and go in. He said he reckoned there was no danger, as it would be covered over with the hay, and there was a watchman about the premises all night. I know that Zantzinger & Co. have had a good deal of liquor on hand for a long time. At the time of, and since the evacuation of the city by the confederates, they had quite a large quantity on hand.

—— —— *Clark*, being duly sworn, says: I have been one of the wharf guards ever since the troops came to Norfolk. A large part of the time I have been on guard at Zantzinger's wharf. Nothing was ever brought there at night to my knowledge, nor have I ever heard of anything being brought there at night. I do not think any contraband goods could have been landed there at night without my hearing or seeing something of it. Such matters have always been mentioned by the members of the guard to each other, and I should probably have known in some way that contraband goods had been landed there, if such had really been the case.

Mr. Dunn: I am U. S. Collector; the license shown me is one issued from my office to Messrs. Zantzinger & Co.; it was issued the 21st of August, 1863; they told me at the time they had a large supply of liquor on hand; they were open and candid in regard to their having large quantities of liquor: they made no effort at concealment.

Col. Dulaney: I have bought a good deal of liquor of Messrs. Zantzinger & Co. within the last four or five months: they have always stated to me that they had large quantities on hand; they sold it publicly, and apparently did not care who knew they had it. [Col. Dulaney is in the regular army of the United States.]

Capt. Croft: Have talked with Messrs. Zantzinger & Co. about their having liquor for sale: asked them if they sold to soldiers; they said they never did; said they had a large amount on hand; there was no sign of concealment.

Mr. Allatt: This January one year ago, was in the store of Zantzinger & Co., saw a great many barrels marked "cider vinegar." Daniels drew whisky from barrels among the lot and handed me a drink: there must have been some seventy or eighty barrels, marked "cider vinegar," which I understood to be filled with whisky.

Captain Drummond: At the time of the evacuation of Norfolk I remember that Zantzinger & Daniels had quite a large quantity of liquor on hand; I think I saw some two hundred barrels in their store, some up stairs, some down.

Lieutenant Wood (recalled): When I called at Messrs. Zantzinger & Co.'s store, I asked them, as I remember, what liquors they had in their *store.* They gave me an inventory which I think is correct. I then asked them what they had in the shed. Daniels replied, "go in there and see for yourself." They sent a clerk in with me. They did not say they had no liquor in the shed; they said nothing about the liquors in the shed till I found it, except "go in and examine for yourself." The first barrel I found under the hay I asked the clerk what it was; he said it was whisky.

The testimony closed here. One hour was required for consultation; verdict at the end of the hour: Fine one thousand dollars, whisky confiscated. It was sold at auction on the public streets of Norfolk, about the 20th of January, for upwards of $14,000. Yes, I say, fourteen thousand dollars. Now, I ask the impartial judgment of any man living, on that testimony, after they had paid their city, State, and United States license, what is there in the case to inflict this punishment? What military order was pretended to be violated? But, you will mark, it was publicly known they had liquor in the shed; the officer knew it. He seems to be playing sharp; asks them "how much they had in the *store?*" They answered correctly. "How much in the shed?" "Go and see; clerk, go with them." Were they criminal in having it to the predjudice of good order and military discipline? Was it smuggled? Look to the record. With the verdict the following order was issued:

HEADQUARTERS PROVOST MARSHAL'S OFFICE,
DISTRICT OF VIRGINIA, NORFOLK, VA., *January* 16, 1864.

Messrs. ZANTZINGER & Co.:

I am ordered to instruct you that you will be allowed to sell your stock of goods now on hand, but you will not be allowed to increase your stock by purchase or otherwise, but will sell out with a view to closing business.

Signed, CHAS. M. WHELDEN,
Lt. Col. and Provost Marshal, Dist. Va.

But the *animus* of General Butler can only be seen by connecting this case with

HODGINS'S CASE.

In November, 1863, Hodgins bought a stock of hardware of a man by the name of Hartshorn, who was trustee for an old firm which failed before the rebellion. The hardware was in a storehouse belonging to William E. Taylor, who was in the rebel army. Mrs. Taylor, his wife, resided in Norfolk. Hartshorn had rented the house from her. Hodgins continued to occupy the house at fifty dollars per month, and paid her that sum for the month of December. Sometime in December Major Moss, the agent of the Treasury Department to collect and take care of abandoned property, called on Hodgins and told him he would probably have to pay the rent to the United States Government. Hodgins replied that he was willing to pay anybody that was entitled; that he had paid that month to Mrs. Taylor in advance, as she was needy. Major Moss took Hodgins's name and left. Between the 15th and 20th of January, Major Moss called on Hodgins and told him he had received instructions from headquarters that the house he occupied was needed for military purposes, and he would have to leave. Hodgins used all the argument he could against leaving; that he had put repairs on the storehouse, that he was not able to move, and that it would cost a large amount to fit up another house. Major Moss called a second time, and the order was peremptory. The young man left; had to pay a Jew $300 for the key of another house; to fix shelving at a cost of $180, and remove ten thousand dollars' worth of small hardware. The house Hodgins was ordered to leave was the best and most eligible business house in the city, on Main, at the head of Market street. Hodgins got into his new house about the 9th of February. The day he left, the Taylor house commenced being fitted up for a liquor store, and in a few days it was occupied by a firm from Boston, with some $25,000 worth of liquors of all kinds, and groceries. About the same time another firm from Boston and another from Lowell, Massachusetts, came in with large assortments of liquors, so that I am safe in saying that in thirty days from the time Zantzinger & Daniels's whiskey was sold, there were $75,000 worth of liquor in Norfolk, in the hands of Bostonians, when a native of Virginia, or any other State, could not get a permit for one gallon.

Put the charge against Zantzinger & Daniels with the order to remove Hodgins out of the house together, and it only proves a fixed determination to close them up, break them up, put $15,000 into the provost marshal's fund, and make a clear track for these Boston men to monopolize the whole business; and Major Moss says he talked with General Butler about requiring Hodgins to remove, and the General pressed his removal, but did not give an actual order. Hodgins went to the provost marshal and tried to get him to interfere. He asked Hodgins if he had a written contract with Major Moss for the house; he said, no. He then said he could do nothing.

Zantzinger is the brother-in-law of Commodore Farragut and a member of the loyal Legislature of Virginia. Daniels is a loyal business man. Hodgins was in the confederate army, but left it at an early day, came home, took the oath, and has behaved himself and claims to be a loyal man.

G. W. SINGLETON'S CASE.

G. W. Singleton was a resident of Nansemond county; was made postmaster on the 16th day of April, 1861, when no other man would take the place under Mr. Lincoln; had two stores, a farm, and seven slaves. When the Union army took Suffolk, he was the first man in the county who went forward immediately and took the oath; moved both stores together into Suffolk; had his dwelling, storehouse, and twelve other small houses on the bank of the river. When Longstreet attacked Suffolk last spring, the Union batteries were erected in Town Square, back of Singleton's houses. His storehouse was blown up and his dwelling and other houses were torn down lest they should take fire and prevent the working of the batteries. Singleton was sent to the mouth of the river, and piloted the magazine boat from the James river to Suffolk. He went back again and piloted up a gun boat. When the gun boat got opposite his farm they were attacked by the rebels, who occupied the farm. Singleton told the Union men to spare nothing; he had there 500 bushels of corn in the crib, 8000 pounds of bacon smoked in his smoke house, with all the other articles a thrifty farmer would have around him. It was all destroyed; not a dollar's worth of buildings, fences, corn, bacon, house, or anything else was left. After the rebels were repulsed he took his wife and children, and $3,500 in money, which was all he had left out of an estate of $40,000, and went to Norfolk. His money was running down, his eldest daughter ready to go to school, and something must be done. When he saw Daniels & Zantzinger's liquor was to be sold in Norfolk, it was natural to suppose the purchasers would be permitted to resell, so he purchased ten barrels, for which he paid $3,325, bought some groceries, and in the course of eight or ten days, opened a store, having paid State, city, and United States license. About seven days after he commenced selling, General Butler's famous order No. 19 came out, requiring all grocery and liquor dealers to obtain a permit therefor at his headquarters. Singleton immediately went to Fort Monroe with Governor Cowper. Cowper stated Singleton's case to Colonel Shafer, chief-of-staff. Colonel Shafer immediately gave an order to Captain Cassell, provost marshal, to grant Singleton a permit to sell groceries and liquors. Singleton returned to Norfolk, and in a few days, as his stock was running down, he made out a requisition for permission to bring from Baltimore liquors and groceries. General Wild signed it. He took it to Captain Cassell at Fort Monroe to get it approved; handed it to Cassel, who pitched it into a pigeon hole. Singleton requested him to sign it; Cassel refused, saying that Singleton had no permit. Singleton assured him that he had. Cassell asked to see it; Singleton handed it to him. He said it was a mistake; it was intended for a permit to keep an eating house. Singleton asked him to look at Colonel Shafer's order; Captain Cassell said he did not know anything about Shafer's order; he would have to wait until Colonel Shafer came home: he would be back perhaps next week, or the week after, or may be not at all. So Singleton went to General Butler and stated his case. General Butler said he would have to wait until Captain Cassell reported the case to him. But Singleton attempted to urge the matter, and General Butler replied, "you want to force me, do you. Now, the less you say the better." So poor Singleton had to leave, his permit taken from him, and there he is, with the residue of his whisky on hand—no permit to sell.

WM. R. JONES'S CASE.

Mr. Jones has resided in Norfolk for twenty years; was a prosperous man, engaged in grocery and liquor business. At commencement of the rebellion was worth perhaps $40,000, partly invested in State and bank stocks, and otherwise where it is mostly unproductive; is a truly loyal man. He made application for a permit to bring in liquors, and was informed by Provost Marshal Whelden that applications must be made directly to General Butler by letter. He went in a few days to see about it, and was informed by Capt. Cassell that the permit was not granted. He went on to Baltimore and called on his return and inquired again. He was informed by same party that no more permits would be granted. Jones asked reason. The reply was General Butler would take the responsibility, and that was the end of it.

A NAMELESS CASE.

A sedate, quiet, honest gentleman, resident in a city I am not permitted to name, was informed that by going to another city I am not permitted to name, and inquire at a certain place, he would find a man, and by paying him he could get a permit to sell liquor and groceries in Norfolk. He went, found the man, and asked for a permit. The reply was, "How much can you pay?" Answered, "Not one dollar." "You can't have the permit." He left, got letters of good standing as to character and loyalty, and took them to General Butler. The General asked him where he lived. "In ———." "But," says the General, "I am giving these permits to natives in Norfolk, to encourage them." "Well," says my friend, "I am a native of Norfolk; only left there a few years ago, and want to go back again." "Well," said the General, "Colonel Shafer, my chief-of-staff, who attends to this business, is absent at present, and when he returns your case shall receive first consideration." The poor man waited ten days, saw three new liquor and grocery firms open up after he made his application, and called on General Butler again, who very politely informed him that Colonel Shafer, his chief-of-staff had not yet returned.

One man in Norfolk, who has been there two or three years has a permit,, and says he got it in such a disgraceful way that he is ashamed to tell how he got it. Another who was known to have money, was accosted one day very politely, I believe, by a gent in uniform, and asked how much he would give to be shown parties who had one of those exclusive permits from whom he could get one third interest in the firm. He replied, "I will give two thousand five hundred dollars to the party showing me the men, and put ten thousand dollars capital into the concern." The middleman replied, "I will see you to-morrow." So on the morrow the papers were all signed, and the two thousand five hundred dollars given.

The liquor business now stands thus in Norfolk. A few men from Boston and Lowell, Mass., have the exclusive monopoly of importing it into the city. All the hotels and restaurants are open to retail, but not at the bars. They have shelves in a room and tables set around. You must take a seat at the table as if eating; the liquor is furnished; you pay twenty-five cents per drink—two dollars for a bottle holding three half pints of common whisky, and three dollars for a bottle of good. The restaurant keepers pay these Boston men three dollars per gallon for whisky that costs in Baltimore from ninety-five to one hundred and five cents, and nine dollars per gallon for whisky that costs two dollars and a half to three dollars per gallon. The poor oyster men must have whisky, they think; some citizens must have, and all the officers and many soldiers will have, let the cost be what it will.

THE GAS WORKS.

I think all the holders of gas stock in Norfolk were disloyal. About the first of July last they stopped making gas; coal run out, and the officers would not take the oath of allegiance in order to get permits to ship more. They continued closed until December, when General Butler issued his order that all the residents in his district should take the oath prescribed in the President's amnesty proclamation. In the order it was stated that every person "to have his rights in any way protected must take and subscribe the oath," &c. The proposition is here plainly inferrable that if they do take and subscribe this oath, their rights of property shall be protected. On the issuing of the order the president and directors, and all the stockholders (except those in rebellion) went forward and took and subscribed the oath, and made immediate preparation to start the gas works, but they were stopped. General Butler seized the whole concern and put them into operation himself, although the president of the company assured him that he could start them in a few days, and would supply all the gas needed. Yet General Butler sent to Lowell for a man and fixtures to repair at a cost of ten thousand dollars, and has now the works in operation, furnishing gas to the city on account of somebody, I don't know whom. I suppose the profits go into the *provost marshal's fund*. He sells the gas at nearly double the price paid in Washington.

In the safe there were upwards of thirteen hundred dollars, which Dr. Cook, the president, desired to take out, but was prohibited and asked to leave it there a few days, and assured that he should have it. But he has not been able to get one cent of it.

Now, I grant all these people owning the gas works were disloyal. Yet they were in effect assured by this order that if they took the oath prescribed they should be protected in their rights. They took the oath, and desired to manufacture their gas. What possible plausibility had Gen. Butler for seizing their gas works and their money and appropriating them? Is the making of gas a part of the suppressing of the rebellion? The fact is, a large amount of the stockholders are widows, old maids, and orphans—all their subsistence is taken from them in one way and another. Many of them were slave owners; their slaves are all gone, and in the language of Dr. Cook, one of their own number, they are only respectable *vagabonds*, and must, many of them who once were wealthy, soon become objects of charity. Then why not live up to the bond we made with them—take the oath and your rights shall be respected? They took the oath; their gas works and money were immediately taken from them. This, I say, with all due deference, is not the way to put down the rebellion.

MRS. TATEM'S CASE.

Sometime in January, Gen. Butler issued an order appointing three commissioners to examine into the condition of the savings banks of Norfolk and Portsmouth, under the plea that the money of the poor of the city had been deposited there, and that the officers had used it and would not pay the depositors. It was believed by those who had some opportunity to know, that the money had been sent to Richmond long ago. So it turned out. But Mrs. Tatem, a widow lady, had two silver cake baskets and some other pieces of silver, belonging to her daughter in Europe, and when the rebel army first came there in 1861, one of her daughters took the silver, placed some napkins around it, and put it in a box and placed it in the vault of the savings bank in Portsmouth. It remained there until Gen. Butler's commissioners went there. Mrs. Tatem called on them and asked them for the silver, but she could not get it. They treated her politely. She called on the provost marshal. He referred her to somebody else, who referred her back to the commissioners, who still refuse to give up the silver. So the silver baskets are gone; she has not been able to get them. I heard the story in Norfolk; it looked impossible. I went to Portsmouth and called at Mrs. Tatem's. She was not at home, but her daughter, a modest young lady of perhaps seventeen or eighteen years, politely asked me into the parlor, and said perhaps she could answer for her mamma. I told her my business; she told me that she placed the silver in the safe herself, and gave the facts substantially as above. She remarked: "We have all taken the oath to the United States, I have three brothers, none of them went into the rebel army, and we are trying to be good citizens," and she added, "but, sir, we have not written to sister what has become of her silver, we are ashamed to let it be known in Europe that our Government is treating us so badly." Gentlemen, upon hearing this, my heart filled. I had a new hope for my country and the Republic. Pure woman, God bless her, she governs the world, and when she makes her allegiance, whether to her husband or her country, she will die before she will expose the shame of her liege.

MR. BILISOLLY

Resided in Portsmouth. Some of the neighboring women took some silver to his house, and put it in the possession of the female members of his family, without his knowledge. The old man is about seventy years of age, and was a director of the savings bank. He was summoned before General Butler, and interrogated as to this silver. The old man knew nothing of it, and so replied. General Butler told him he was a liar, and he would put him in Fort Norfolk on bread and water until he learned to tell the truth. The old man replied, "Sir, I am your prisoner, or you should not address me thus." The old man was put into the fort without a blanket, on the cold floor, and is still there. I received a letter from one of his daughters, a good Union woman, in which she says: "My dear mother sent to Fort Monroe a nice new cotton mattress, a pair of blankets, one comforter, one pair of sheets, and one pillow, which were never delivered to father." At the time Bilisolly was arrested, they found in his house, deposited as above stated, in one bundle, a large soup ladle, two silver mugs, two pairs of sugar tongs, half a dozen old fashioned table spoons, with other table spoons and tea spoons; and one other bundle, somewhat larger, consisting of twenty-seven pieces, from soup ladle to salt spoon.

Bilisolly is an eccentric man; he laid in liquors at the birth of his children, as well as at their wedding. When his youngest daughter was born, now twenty years ago, he had a surplus of one dozen bottles of wine and eight bottles of brandy, which he corked up and laid aside, to break when she married. But the wine and brandy went with the silver, and, I suppose, if not since separated, have gone into the *provost marshal's fund* together.

I desire to call attention to the fact that the public have been fully informed of General Butler's prompt and even severe dealing with the officers of the savings bank, and the sending of them to Fort Hatteras and Norfolk; of the seizure of the gas works and running it on his own account, but they have never heard one word about what became of the silver in Bilisolly's house, Mrs. Tatem's silver baskets, or the thirteen hundred dollars in the safe in the gas works.

NEWSPAPERS AND MAGAZINES.

In February, General Butler issued an order asking for bids until the first of March, for the privilege of furnishing newspapers and periodicals in his district, by the month, promising to award the monopoly to the "*successful*" bidder, not to the highest. An old Jew by the name of Bohn was the successful bidder, at the price of $600 per month. All other dealers were closed up, among whom were Mahew & Brother, who had a news store in Norfolk, had paid a license to the city, State, and United States Governments, and were doing a fair business. They supposed the order did not refer to Norfolk, and as they had paid their internal revenue license, they continued their business. Soon, however, they were summoned to Old Point before Captain Cassell. When they got there, Cassell asked them if they took the papers. They replied, "We do." Said he, "Do you read them?" Reply, "We do." "Then," said he, "do you understand what you read?" Answer, "We do, or suppose we do." Said he, "Do you live in Norfolk?" "Yes." "Did you see the order awarding the privilege of supplying this district with papers and magazines to Mr. Bohn?" They answered, "We did." "Well," said he, "that order was issued by command of General Butler, and if you persist in bringing papers into this department, I will use all my influence to have you punished." Thus, American citizens from Pennsylvania, who have resided in Norfolk near two years, are cut off from business. They paid the United States Government $18 45 for internal revenue license alone, with a solemn undertaking on the part of the Government to protect them in their business. And this in addition to what they would pay on income; but the income has gone into the *provost marshal's fund.*

THE DOGS.

It was supposed that all the sources whence money could be derived were exhausted. But a happy thought occurred as deep contemplation occupied the mind of the soldier; not like that which absorbed Alexander when he wept because there was not another world to conquer, but "where was more money?" The Dogs! happy thought; dogs occupy a tender place in the affections of the old and young and middle aged, and there is a good supply in the two cities from the poodle to the butcher's bull dog. So the following order was issued, *verbatim:*

HEADQUARTERS, NORFOLK AND PORTSMOUTH,
Norfolk, Va., March 7, 1864.

General Order, No. 6.

Let every fourth dog in the district be killed. The Provost Marshals of Norfolk and Portsmouth will see this order executed. By command of Brigadier General E. A. Wild.

GEORGE H. JOHNSON,
Capt. and Assistant Adjutant General.

CHARLES E. WHELDEN,
Lieut. Col. and Provost Marshal.

This decree was very general, not like that of Herod's in regard to children. But every fourth dog, generally, without reference to age, sex, or condition. This order produced great sensation; it was so general. How would they ascertain the fourth dog? At last my friend Peter Whitehurst declared that all the dogs in the department would have to be killed but three, then there would be no fourth dog left. This produced great consternation among the old maids and the young sportsmen for their poodles and pointers, so they rushed to the headquarters and inquired for an interpretation of the order, when they were very politely informed by the following answer: "Ladies and gentlemen, we do not desire to hurt a hair on your dog's back. It is only to increase the *provost marshal's fund* that the order is made. All of you who will pay two dollars to the provost marshal, get a license for your dog, and a collar and put on his neck, can keep him, to comfort your declining years and youthful sports." On the 23d of March near $1,500 had been paid in. I did not learn whether a Boston friend had the monopoly of selling dog collars. But the order must be carried out by way of paying the money. The veteran soldiers—white soldiers—were detailed to hunt them up and bring them in for redemption.

When I landed in Norfolk the other day, I went up Main street to the hotel. After I passed the provost marshal's office, I met a veteran soldier leading with a rope a fine, noble countenanced pointer dog. The poor fellow looked restive. He seemed to recognize a friend in me, and ran around me bringing the rope around my limbs. I extricated myself and told him I was only a civilian. A little further on I met another soldier with a medium-sized cur, with his head and tail down, showing his teeth a little, looked surly and as much as to say, "I did'nt know that this war was about dogs; I don't care a —— which side whips," or such sentiment as might be expected from a mean cur. A little further on I met another soldier with a line around a little dog's neck; he was between the spaniel and the poodle—white wool—but dirty; his chin was close on the ground, his eyes upturned meekly, and wagging his tail gently as he went along. A juvenile freedman, who was standing on the pavement, said, "little doggie, if you don't get two dollars, Massa Butler will take de wag out ob your tail."

HOWARD ASSOCIATION.

When the yellow fever raged in Norfolk and Portsmouth, in 1855, the good people of the neighboring cities sent in a large amount of money to some gentlemen who formed a society, under the name of the Howard Association. There was $60,000 left after the fever had abated. They were chartered by the Legislature of Virginia for the purpose of taking care of and supporting the orphans made by the yellow fever, and for other benevolent objects, when that was accomplished. The members of the Board have faithfully preserved the fund, using the interest for the purpose. There are some twelve or fifteen of the orphans which are still a charge upon them. Last year they had a small surplus of interest which they devoted to the poor. The money is all invested in loans, secured by mortgages on real estate and bonds with personal security. Some of the directors are disloyal, but the evidences of the debt are on record, and they are faithfully discharging their duty. On the 22d of March, General Butler issued an order, directing a committee of three, two of them officers on his staff, one a civilian of recent settlement in the city, to take possession of the assets of the association. On the 22d, Captain Edgar called on the secretary of the association, and demanded of him and obtained all the assets of the association; and on the 23d ordered all the board to meet him at the provost marshal's office.

General Butler, with the same propriety and more, might seize the assets of Girard College, or that of any professorship in Harvard University, for taking care of the poor in Norfolk and Princess Anne counties.

I will here make a remark in regard to the great clamor through the North about General Butler taking charge of the poor. He has a preacher going around trying to convince the people that General Butler is a very proper man; he is so liberal to the poor, thus using Heaven's liveried missionaries to make his conduct palatable. But General Butler can never get the co-operation of the Union people of Norfolk in any enterprise, however benevolent, while it is under the management of members of his staff and associates, simply because they have no confidence in them.

I desire to put to rest this clamor about the Government taking care of the poor in Norfolk and Princess Anne counties, and the two cities. Ever since the Union troops occupied the cities of Norfolk and Portsmouth, the military have had possession of the ferry and boats between the two cities, using them for its own profit and benefit, collecting tolls from all civilians, and transporting Government troops and property. This ferry belongs to the two cities; they have not received one dollar from it. The military has got it all. The receipts of the ferry before the war, amounted to from $15,000 to $18,000 per annum. Since the military has had it I am satisfied that if the Government had paid for its use at the same rate that any similar service is paid for in the North, it would yield at least forty thousand dollars per annum, which is twice the sum appropriated for taking care of the poor. But this committee for taking care of the poor are holding meetings, are abusing the Union men for not rallying around them, and trying to get up the idea that there are no Union men in Norfolk. The Union men won't rally under such leadership. The poor are from the oyster men, who are so taxed and fined that they can't make a living. The poor in the county are, many of them, made so by the destruction and plunder of the helpless, in military raids. A highly intelligent gentleman, and now a loyal member of the Virginia State Convention, told me that for three weeks after General Wild made his celebrated raid in Princess Anne, he could stand on the portico of his house and trace the track of the raid for ten miles by the turkey buzzards, feeding on the carrion made by destruction of animal life. Union men and widows shared the same fate; all they had was taken or destroyed, and thus many of the poor are made. I forbear facts and incidents. Many of the poor are the wives and children of rebels, either killed or now serving in the rebel army. The Union men have urged that the rich rebels left behind should take care of them. It was urged as a distinct proposition, that the rents of the property of rebels who were in rebellion, and at home, should go to their support. It was urged that Tazwell Taylor, the commissioner to procure a rebel loan in Norfolk, and who was a member of Magruder's staff while the rebels were there, and who took $15,000 of the rebel loan, should be taxed or compelled to contribute $15,000 to take care of the rebel poor. But strange to say, this same Tazwell remained a bitter rebel to the last, was General Naglee's closest companion, and was called in by General Butler to consult about the civil government of Norfolk.

Tazwell left the city and removed to Baltimore, without ever contributing one cent, as far as General Butler is concerned, for support of rebel poor; and now the support of the poor is made a scapegoat in the estimation of all General Butler's admirers, and a salvo for seizing and taxing everything; and because the Union men who have liberally drained their pockets to support the poor, will not come forward and follow the dictates of Captain Edgar, in whom they have no confidence, they are stigmatized as rebels, and forsooth, there is no loyalty in the city.

It is now too late to lay any contribution on rebel property holders in the cities to support the poor. General Butler has required them all to take the oath of allegiance, with promise of protection, and the promise ought to be kept. The Union poor can be supported by the Union people, if the avenues of industry and enterprise are left open for them to work; but if part are taxed to fill the coffers of the *provost marshal's fund*, and others prohibited from following their avocations because they are in the way of Boston favorites, they will all soon be paupers and vagabonds. The rebel poor, whose friends and protectors are in the rebel army, must be cared for, either by cutting off their heads, sending them across the lines to their protectors, selling rich rebels' property who are in rebellion, and supporting them out of the proceeds, or the United States Government must support them. These are simple propositions.

The policy of supporting the poor out of rebel property was partially introduced. But when General Butler came it was all broken up. The houses were needed for his officers and Boston friends, who are occupying them free of rent.

THE WOOD BUSINESS.

Shipping fire wood is an extensive and profitable business in Norfolk and that section. After General Butler went there the natives found it difficult to get permits—Bostonians got them. I will give a case.

CAPTAIN CROWEL AND B. & J. BAKER

Had a wrecking vessel which had been sunk. They raised it, partly refitted it, and loaded it with wood, with a view to send the vessel to New York to complete some part of the rigging. They went to General Wild for a permit. He is the military governor of the city. Upon their first call they were refused a permit. They called a second time, in a week after the first. They had one hundred and seventy-five cords of wood loaded, and urged their case; their boat being a wrecking vessel, they stated that if they met a vessel on the way in distress, they would throw their wood overboard and go to her relief, &c. They made a strong case, but the General, however, refused; said he had granted all the permits he thought it prudent to grant, but perhaps if they would go to some of the gentlemen who had permits, they would get permission to ship on their permit. They went to a Boston man by the name of Bishop, who had a permit to ship four thousand six hundred cords. They asked him for a permit, and he consented. One hundred and seventy-five cords at $3 50 per cord at one per cent would be $6 12. They asked Mr. Bishop what they must pay. He replied, "You know I have to pay one per cent." They handed him $25 00, and asked them if that would be satisfactory. He replied it would. Crowel is an old man, and a true Union man. B. & J. Baker are northern men and have been there for many years, engaged as wreckers. I don't know their politics, if they have any.

SALE OF CORN.

It is difficult to get a permit to send corn out of the department. I find no fault with the rule, but some do get permits. There were some twelve to fifteen thousand bushels of corn to be sold for the benefit of the freedmen, being their share of a lot raised last year. The money was going to them. A native by the name of Patterson had a contract for delivering corn to the Government, at $1 25 per bushel, at Norfolk. Some man from the North said he had a permit to ship, so he was ready to buy. Patterson and the Northern man (I don't know where he was from) were competitors at the sale. The corn was run up to $1 12 per bushel, and bought by Patterson, much to the chagrin of the stranger, who remarked that he "did not know why Patterson bid so much, he had no permit to ship." I merely mention this to teach gentlemen who express so much sympathy for the poor freedman how they might have given him bread and raiment, and done no injustice to any person. The Government wanted corn, and General Wild gave Patterson the contract. Patterson turned the corn over to the Government, perhaps without handling, at $1 25 per bushel. Why could not the party superintending the sale have had it turned over to the Government at $1 25? The profits of Patterson would have gotten many, many comforts for the little freedman. But then there would have been no hope of speculation to the gentleman with the permit.

BUCK & CO.

This company is composed of Joseph A. Buck, Isaac M. Dennison, Peter H. Whitehurst, and Charles Whitehurst. This firm did a large business in dry goods and groceries, old iron, pewter, lead, brass, copper, old rope, sails, and grain. They were engaged in it before the rebellion. The vessel E. C. Knight, loaded with lumber, stranded on the beach of Princess Anne county, about the first of January last. The underwriters sold the cargo to the highest bidder. Quartermaster Godwin became the purchaser, and employed a Captain Caffee, a resident near the lumber, to haul it over the beach to a landing on Currituck Sound, where it could be loaded and brought to Norfolk. Great expedition was required, lest by rise of wind and tide the lumber should be lost. Caffee employed above one hundred hands, and got over one hundred and fifty-nine thousand feet of lumber, for which he was to get twelve dollars per thousand feet. He knew it would be some time before he could get his money, and they desired to have some groceries and salt to salt their pork. He called on Buck & Co., who had engaged to take two vessels and bring down the lumber, to furnish these articles to pay the hands for their labor, and wait with him until he got his money from the Government. Thereby he would be accommodated and they would make a profit. So Buck & Co. called on Quartermaster Godwin for permission, and he referred them to the provost marshal. The application was in these words:

"Gen. Wild: Sir—We respectfully ask permission to ship to Knott's Island, per schooner Georgia, to be sold to men that have been working to save Government property on the sea-beach, the following articles: one hundred sacks salt, ten barrels flour, five barrels syrup, two barrels sugar, one box tobacco, and two bags of coffee."

They were going to take two schooners and another cargo of same quantity on a similar permit.

They went to Provost Marshal Whelden, presented their permit to his clerk, Tilden, who was sitting by the side of the provost marshal, showed him that they had taken the oath, and had paid their license. He endorsed it and handed it to the provost marshal, who signed it. Buck then asked him to whom they should take it next. The clerk replied,

"That is all right; every officer in the department would respect that." Buck, to be sure, repeated in substance the same remark, and received the same answer. They started on their journey and were arrested some fifteen or twenty miles from the city, and brought back by order of the provost marshal, who ordered them before the provost judge, to try them and confiscate their property for attempting to run the blockade. They waited ten days before a trial could be obtained, their vessels lying there. They had their trial, the facts turned out as above stated, and they were released, and went immediately to the vessels. Before they reached the store they were arrested again for having old brass and copper on hand belonging to the Government. They immediately appeared before the provost judge. He was on another case and they could get no trial for some seven days. They were finally tried and acquitted.

They were thus detained about seventeen days with their vessels, at a cost of about twenty dollars per day, and had to give up their adventure. Since that time they have made five different applications for shipping the produce on hand, consisting of rags, cotton, old iron, copper, brass, lead, pewter, bees-wax, old grease, bristles, old rope, sails, and wood, of which they have about ten thousand dollars worth on hand, all of which have been refused. Finally, Buck wrote a statement to General Butler of himself and his connection with Whitehurst, alleging his loyalty, the purity of his intentions, that General Wild had stated there was a cloud hanging over his character, and offering to prove as loyal and upright a character as any man in the department, civil or military, and asking that he might be placed on an equal footing with other men. General Butler referred the letter to General Wild, and General Wild made on the letter the following endorsements:

"HEADQUARTERS, DEPARTMENT OF VA. AND N. C.,
"*February* 24, 1864.

"Respectfully referred to General Wild, to know what is the objection to Mr. Buck.

"By command of Major General Butler.

"H. C. CLARK,
"*Captain and A. D. C.*'

"HEADQUARTERS, NORFOLK AND PORTSMOUTH, VA.,
NORFOLK, VA., *February* 28, 1864

Respectfully return, with a reference to page 2d, part II. These goods were ostensibly sent for the use only of a gang of workmen and their families engaged on the ocean shore where there ought to be salt enough for their limited purposes. In effect, they were to go beyond our lines to a neighborhood noted for disloyalty of the worst fame, "guerrillas," between which point and Richmond there would be no obstacle to the transportation of every pound, and these invoices would pay richly for the trouble. Also, with a reference to page 3d, line 3d. Buck knew well enough the character of Caffee, a guerrilla himself, and brother, and brother-in-law, uncle, and cousin to several other guerrillas. Buck could very easy surmise what sort of a gang of workmen Caffee would get together. Yet he was ready to place in his hands such invoices of goods as these. Also, with reference to page 2d, line 99, &c., &c. Buck has done business enough here to know that he could not travel all over the department on the word of a provost marshal's clerk, nor on a mere certificate that he had taken the oath; that the permission from the commanding officer, which he had to obtain for every one of his imports and exports, was vastly more necessary for trading over the lines. Also, with reference to page 2d, line 3d, Judge Stackpole—verdict, released vessels and goods from confiscation, but did not let them resume the voyage. Buck then, for the first time, came in to ask me for that permit. It was disapproved at once. Also, with a reference to page 3d, line 3d. This relates to large quantities of old junk that Buck tried to export, containing brass, copper, &c., stolen from Navy Yards, &c. Also with reference to page 1st, line 24th; Buck here admits a fact which Whitehurst denied and confessed again half a dozen times in so many minutes, when questioned by me. Buck had a large quantity of old junk, rags, cotton, and stoves to export. Finding all his permits retained until the question of theft was settled he brought Whitehurst to his aid, who in three different applications tried to ship Buck's goods. These were identified by the harbor police in spite of Whitehurst's repeated assertions and angry protestations. Shifting of imports and permits from one party to another is inadmissible in these troublesome times, and should subject both parties to a stoppage of all further privileges. This Buck case grew worse with

Whitehurst's help. I made up my mind that Buck's acquisitiveness was much larger than his loyalty and rectitude. Moreover, I learned his partner in Baltimore. Denison, has been from the first a known secessionist, active in word if not in deed. This I gathered from Whitehurst himself. I therefore enclosed all the papers in the case, February 12th, and forwarded them to Major R. L. Davis, Acting Adjutant General. They were returned with his letter of transmittal.

'PROVOST MARSHAL'S OFFICE, HEADQUARTERS,
FORT MONROE, *Va.*, *February* 16, 1864.

Brig. Gen. Wild, Norfolk, Va.:

I am directed by the Major General commanding to return to you the enclosed application of Buck & Co., and to state that the disposition of them is left to your discretion. Your decision in the matter will be *final.*

I am, General, very respectfully, your obedient servant,
JOHN CASSELLS,
Captain and A. D. C.'

"I at once decided to disapprove all of Buck's permits for the future, that he is too slippery for this department. That he be at liberty to sell out at his leisure, and should have permission to return to Baltimore and indulge his trading propensities in a safe field. I shall follow the same course with Peter Whitehurst.

Respectfully submitted,
EDWARD A. WILD,
Brig. Gen. Commanding.

"General Wild's action approved.
(Signed,) BENJ. F. BUTLER."

This is a paper of grave import, and contains grave charges.

After all these endorsements were made, the paper was sent to Buck by General Butler. There is evidently a bad feeling in General Wild's mind towards Buck and Whitehurst. They know of no reason for it, except it grew out of a transaction connected with General Wild's celebrated raid into North Carolina and Princess Anne county. It was this: While near where Captain Caffee lives, General Wild came to the house owned by a man by the name of White, who was a captain in the confederate service. General Wild arrested Mrs. White, the wife, as a hostage for something, I don't know what. She was in a delicate situation. Her daughter, a young girl of about nineteen years of age, stepped forward and said, "General, you cannot take my mother, take me." He took the daughter and set fire to the house, and burnt everything in it, with all the nick nacks of an expectant mother. In two days afterward Mrs. White was confined, the daughter was taken a prisoner. They had not proceeded far until they came to Colonel Mix, of New York, with his regiment. The Colonel and his men, seeing the young girl in possession of the colored troops, interfered, and declared they were sent to protect persons and property, and were going to rescue the girl. The men and officers in both commands became highly excited, and were about coming into conflict, when the girl stepped forward and said: "Men, don't shed blood on my account; they have not mistreated me; my honor is untarnished; I am here in place of my mother." The angry blood cooled, the girl was carried to Norfolk, and kept there in the second story of General Wild's headquarters some three weeks, her mother, in the meantime, lying at the point of death; and by the efforts of Captain Caffee, aided by Buck and Whitehurst, the girl was released, I think through General Butler. This interference may have been their sin, which cast them from favor. Captain Caffee is an old sea captain, resides in Princess Anne county, is a man of substance and energy, and has relations by blood and marriage in the confederate army, but who has not? I cannot learn that Caffee is a guerrilla, or ever has been one. He is back and forward frequently, I understand, at Norfolk, and if Caffee is a guerrilla, as declared by General Wild, he, having the command, certainly ought to arrest him and try him as such.

General Wild declares in this endorsement that these goods (in the schooner) "in effect were to go beyond our lines." How does he know this? He broadly asserts it; yet he kept them for ten days before he tried the parties, and they were acquitted in his own court, by his own judge, on the testimony of the clerk in the provost marshal's office. Caffee and his men were good enough to trust by the quartermaster to bring a large amount of lumber across the bar, when great dispatch was required to prevent loss. If sufficiently faithful to work for the Government where, if they did not work, it would incur great loss, why object to their having a little salt, sugar, and coffee?

These same men, headed by Caffee, have saved for the Government, since that time, about half a million dollars' worth of property from vessels wrecked on the same coast where these goods were destined. And yet this Caffee and his men are denounced as guerrillas.

General Wild charges that "in page third, line third, this relates to large quantities of junk that Buck had to export, containing brass, copper, &c., stolen from Navy, &c." He says he retained all these things until the question of *theft* was settled. Is not that question settled? Were not they summoned before Judge Stackpole, and kept there seven days, and General Wild notified of the fact that they were not guilty, but proved themselves innocent? But Peter Whitehurst denied and confessed a half dozen times the same thing in that many minutes. He learned that Buck's acquisitiveness was larger than his loyalty, and his partner in Baltimore was a rebel; and finally, in his last endorsement, he gives him the privilege to sell out at his leisure and return to Baltimore, and made same order as to Peter Whitehurst.

Now, gentlemen, without repetition, I refer you to the record. General Wild says shifting permits is inadmissible. Yet he advises it in the case of the wood permit, where a Boston friend profited four hundred per cent. by it. Comment is unnecessary.

Peter H. Whitehurst is a native of Virginia, a man of high character, and as loyal a man as lives. The firm to which he belongs has paid more than three thousand dollars for the support of the poor and the Union cause, since our troops occupied Norfolk. Charles Whitehurst is a member of the loyal Virginia Senate, a Christian gentleman, and as pure a man, I think, as I ever met. Buck stands as high, I am informed, as an honorable merchant, as any in Baltimore; his loyalty undoubted. Denison, Buck's partner in Baltimore, was a secessionist in April, 1861. In June he joined one of the Union aid associations in Baltimore. In July, 1863, when Lee invaded Maryland, six months' volunteers were called for. Young Creamer was a clerk in some institution in which Denison was a director. After Creamer left, Denison moved that his company vote him fifty dollars bounty, and keep his place open for him until his return.

This is the class of men stricken down and all the avenues of trade shut up to them, charged with theft, after the General knew they had been acquitted, notified to sell their goods to some other person who would make the speculation by transportation, I suppose. Is this right; is it just, that these men, two of them living in Norfolk, with large families to support, and who have lost largely by the rebellion, should thus be blasted by the caprice of a commanding general? Peter Whitehurst had a slave named Charles, worth fifteen hundred dollars before the war. Charles remained with him until the order came to enlist colored men. Whitehurst went to Charles, although he was not free, and told him, "Charles, you now have a chance to fight for the freedom of your race. Go and join a colored regiment and show yourself a man." Charles said: "Master, I want to stay with you." "No," said Peter, "your country needs you more than I do, go." He went, and is now a soldier, and Peter has never made any demand for service or bounty. This is a Virginia Union man.

YELLOW PINE AND SHIP KNEES.

It is reported that one party from Boston has a permit from General Butler to cut all the yellow pine and ship knees in his district. This is a large operation and may amount to millions. They have commenced cutting all the timber from some farms below Norfolk on the Bay, sawing it into lumber and wood. These farms belong to resident secessionists who reside on their land, who have not taken up arms, nor are their lands liable to confiscation; and they have taken the oath under General Butler's order with the promise of protection. The timber is all cut down, landmarks destroyed, and the farms rendered valueless, to a great extent, for want of timber. I have no objection, where the Government needs lumber, and timber is on land liable to confiscation, to its being cut and used. Nor would it have been very objectionable that when a man owns timber, and is a rebel, and has not taken the oath, to take his timber for Government purposes. But when a man has taken the oath with a promise of protection, the Government is bound to protect him.

THE NEW REGIME.

This is the title of a new daily newspaper, published in Norfolk under the auspices of General Butler. *New Regime* means new government, or order of things. Newspaper enterprises generally depend on private capital and enterprise. But the *New Regime* had two printing establishments, engines, presses, and type seized, belonging to men who had taken the oath. A restaurant keeper was turned out of the house he occupied because it was needed for military purposes—the quartermaster was required to detail hands from Government shops to repair engines and do carpenters' work to the amount of seven hundred and seventeen dollars and forty-five cents, which was charged to the United States Government, and Mr. Chase will have the money to provide to pay, to repair the engines and do carpenter work, to get ready for editing the *New Regime*. Then Captain Clark, one of General Butler's staff, was detailed with a civilian from Boston to edit the paper. Sixty printers—soldiers from the army—were detailed and sent to the office, thirty of them were chosen and now are acting as type setters, printers, and engaged in various ways in getting out the paper, and receiving their pay and rations from the United States Goverment; one of the editors paid as an officer. Suppose these printers to be all veterans, and if they are not veterans will have to take their place in the field. The Government, State and Federal, are paying now, seven hundred dollars bounty, besides clothing.

The *New Regime* stands as to cost to the country per annum, about thus:

For bounty to 30 soldiers, at $700	$21,000 00
Pay, clothing, and subsistence of 30 soldiers, at $30 per month	10,800 00
Cost of repairs to engines and carpenter work	717 46
Pay of Captain Clarke, about	1,800 00
	34,317 46

Captain Clark is on detached duty, and is entitled to commutation for rent, fuel, light, and rooms.

The editor's business notice is as follows: "The job printing department of this office is the most complete in Virginia, and as all our presses are run by steam power, we can afford to execute all kinds of work at the lowest possible price. Send orders to No. 33 Market street, corner of Commerce." Kept up as the *New Regime* is by the Federal Government, at the tune of $34,000 per annum, wearing out the engines, press, and type of men who had taken the oath under promise of protection, it would be supposed that they could do work cheaply. "But there is no need of these soldiers now." For that I cannot say. On the night of the 21st of March, the rebels came within eight miles of Norfolk and destroyed a considerable amount of Government property, and on the night of the 23d, they were within four miles of Norfolk. Rebels are running the lines almost daily. The printer soldier cannot attend to keeping guard or protecting property, were they to do so, this Boston gentleman could not do his work so cheaply.

The object of this newspaper is to create a sink to absorb as much as possible of the *provost marshal's fund* by way of advertisements. Nearly three fourths of it is filled with military orders as advertisements. Also, to prove that the civil government of Virginia should be abolished in General Butler's department and military rule substituted. I called the attention of the Secretary of War to some of the usurpations at Norfolk. Among other things, to the one per cent. on merchandise that was shipped into the department. The *New Regime* takes up the gauntlet, and in his issue of the 7th of March, he devotes nearly three columns to prove that the civil government ought to be abolished and military substituted in General Butler's department. Defending the one per cent. charge, he denounces the opposition to it as the "*howl from a semi-loyal government.*" It is exceedingly offensive to those who have imperiled all, and are still doing all in their power to advance the great cause of the country, to be denounced by a mere parasite as semi-loyal. No man's name appears as editor of the paper.

There are two daily newspapers in Norfolk and Portsmouth with a capacity to do all the printing required by the department.

THE MARKETS.

They have undertaken to regulate the price of articles sold in market. I here give the military order containing the bill of prices:

"HEADQUARTERS NORFOLK AND PORTSMOUTH,
NORFOLK, VA., *February* 11, 1864.

Special Order, No. 30.

The following are established as the maximum prices at which the articles enumerated below may be sold in the markets, shops, stalls, or other places at Norfolk or Portsmouth.

Any person who shall be convicted of selling at higher rates will be punished according to the discretion of the provost marshal, and his produce shall be forfeited.

The only currency will be that permitted by the Government of the United States.

First quality bacon, per lb	$0 16
Second quality bacon	12½
Hams per lb	17
Shoulders, per lb	12½
Fresh beef, per lb	
Fresh sirloin steak, per lb	15
Fresh round steak, per lb	15
Fresh roasting pieces, per lb	15
Fresh coarse pieces, per lb	8
Lard, per lb	18
Butter, per lb	35 to 45
Eggs, per dozen	30
For all kinds of poultry dressed	13
Meal, per lb	2½
Sweet potatoes, per peck	30
Beans, per quart	15
Spots, live, per dozen	30
Spots, salt, per dozen	15
Turkeys and geese, apiece, alive	1 00
Oysters, per quart	15
Oysters, shell, per bushel	50
Lynn Haven, per bushel	75
Cabbage, large, per head	15
Cabbage, small, per head	3 to 8
Roast pigs	50cts. to 1 00
First quality mutton, per lb	15
Second quality mutton per lb	12½
Bread, four ounces per loaf	5
Croakers and drum-head fish, per lb	5
Blue and drum fish, per lb	10
Sheepshead fish, per lb	10
Spanish mackerel, per lb	10
Wood, pine, per cord	3 50
Wood, hard, per cord	4 50
Coal, per ton	11 00
Apples, per barrel	5 00

All groceries not mentioned above, ten per cent. above Baltimore prices.

The above prices will be altered from time to time as the change of season and state of market may require.

By command of Brig. Gen. E. A. Wild:

GEORGE H. JOHNSON,
Capt. and Asst. Adj. Gen.

All conversant with the prices paid in the Eastern markets for similar articles will at once observe that the prices here established are far below the price of any other market. Groceries ten per cent. on Baltimore prices—they paid, when this bill was established, five per cent. to United States Government, one per cent. to General Butler, and at least two and one half per cent. freight, cooperage, &c., making eight and one half per cent.—one and one half per cent. is left for profit.

I herewith give a letter from a Princess Anne county farmer as the best commentary on the market prices:

"PRINCESS ANNE COUNTY, VIRGINIA,
March 22, 1864.

SIR: We think the farmers in the vicinity of Norfolk are very unjustly imposed upon by having the prices fixed upon our market produce by the military authorities.

In the first place, we have to pay higher for our seeds and fertilizers than ever before, say thirty-three per cent., and in addition to that we have to pay five per cent. in Baltimore and one per cent. at Old Point on all the seeds and implements we bring from Baltimore. Labor is higher, and we have suffered from depredations committed by a class of roving whites and blacks, who have stolen our fowl, potatoes, and even some of the horses. Now, to be compelled to take such prices as some military men may dictate, and those prices not more than one half of what is paid in Baltimore, it cannot be claimed as a military necessity. We have to pay the grocers and dry goods men such prices as they may see fit to ask us. Now, why select the farmers and compel them to sell at fixed prices? If the pay of the military who have brought their families here will not support them, let them ask the Government for increase of pay, and not rob the poor farmer.

An ever loyal farmer,

JNO. NEWTON.

To Gov. PIERPOINT, Alexandria, Va."

I do not know Mr. Newton, but this is only one of numerous letters I have received on this and similar subjects.

This all proves one of two things, either the incapacity of the officers who undertake to regulate this subject, or a determination to have the articles produced in market for less than their value. It is immaterial to me to which cause it is attributable.

CASE OF CHAS. W. BUTTS.

Mr. Butts is a lawyer in the city of Norfolk. Gen. Wild made an order confiscating the estate of a man in Portsmouth by the name of Williams. Williams was a rebel, but took the oath under the promise of protection. He heard before he took the oath that the military, with some Boston friends, coveted his dwelling house and handsome furniture. Shortly after taking the oath, an order was made confiscating his property. Williams then (being in delicate health) sent his certificate of having taken the oath prescribed by Gen. Butler, claiming his protection, to General Wild, who kept the certificate and endorsed on the back of it "oath revoked," and ordered the officers in whose possession the books kept for the purpose of recording names, dates, and residence of persons taking the oath, and in which Williams's name was recorded, to erase from them all evidence of Williams's having taken the oath, which was done. Williams, with his wife and children, were turned out of their own house into the streets of Portsmouth, on the 22d of March last, during the prevalence of one of the most terrible snow storms I ever witnessed.

Butts, not in a professional capacity, but as an act of mere justice, wrote the following letter to Attorney General Bates at Washington, accompanied by a copy of Gen. Wild's order of confiscation:

"NORFOLK, VIRGINIA.

"Hon. EDWARD BATES,
Attorney General, Washington, D. C.:

SIR: I have felt it my duty on several occasions to communicate certain facts to you, but have desisted from writing, knowing that your present duties are so onerous that you have but little time to look after such matters. But when a brigadier general of the army takes the civil law in his own hands, and orders real estate to be confiscated without legal cause, totally disregarding the laws of the country as this man Wild has, I feel constrained to write. General Wild, as you are aware, is the military commander of the respective cities of Norfolk and Portsmouth, who, in my opinion, (and I have had considerable military experience,) is not a fit and proper person to be provost marshal over white people. What I wish to complain of is the following order:

[Copy.] PROVOST MARSHAL'S OFFICE,
PORTSMOUTH, VIRGINIA, *March* 9, 1864.

"Mr. JOHN WILLIAMS,
Portsmouth, Virginia:

"By order of Brigadier General Wild, your entire estate is confiscated to the use of the United States Government.

You will furnish the bearer, Corporal Prime, of this office, a list of houses and tenements now in your possession, and vacate the premises you now occupy on or before the 19th of March.

DAN. MESSINGER,
Provost Marshal.

Mr. Williams resides in Portsmouth with his family, and has taken the oath of allegiance under the President's proclamation. If consistent with your views or duties you will greatly oblige by giving this letter your attention as soon as possible.

Very respectfully, your obedient servant,
G. W. BUTTS."

Judge Bates endorsed the letter and sent it to the Secretary of War. He endorsed it and sent it to General Butler. General Butler endorsed it and sent it to General Wild. Wild sent for Butts, asked him if he wrote the letter. Butts said he did; handed Butts a copy to read; and after reading asked him if it was a correct copy. Butts told him it was. Then Butts was shortly afterwards handed an order banishing him from the department. He went to General Butler and complained; asked Butler to rescind it. Among other things Butler told him he was in trouble with him, (General Butler,) and took from a pigeon hole a letter which Butts had written to the President, informing him of the dollar charge on persons going in and out of General Butler's department, which the President had referred to General Butler, and told Butts he was a dangerous man; he would not interfere with General Wild's order. So Butts had to leave, and at this writing is an exile from the home of his adoption and professional business, sitting in my office.

Who is Butts? He is a native of New Jersey, a republican in politics; the first political speech he ever made was advocating Mr. Lincoln's election. He was the second man volunteered in his county in the three months' service; was among the first who crossed from Washington to Alexandria when the lamented Ellsworth fell in that city. He served as a private; was in the New Jersey reserve corps, commanded by General Runyon at the time of the battle of Bull Run. When his term was out he returned home. He raised thirty men at once and joined Colonel Harlan's independent regiment, now the 11th Pennsylvania cavalry, and was commissioned 1st lieutenant, and served with distinction on the

Peninsula, between James and York rivers. Butts has many certificates of which any young man ought to be proud, for acts of daring and gallantry on the field. I will quote the endorsement of Colonel Spear, the gallant commander of his regiment, on his request to resign:

"HEADQUARTERS 11TH PENNSYLVANIA CAVALRY,
(Near Portsmouth, Virginia,) *October* 4, 1863.

"Approved and recommended. I am fully aware of the reasons which compel this applicant to offer his resignation. I have known him to take the field when he was more fitted to be in bed, and was prompted to do so by pure energetic motives. He has on many occasions distinguished himself in action: brave, cool, and determined as an officer, urbane, polite and gentlemanly as a citizen. I shall deeply deplore his loss to my regiment.

(Signed,) SAMUEL P. SPEAR,
Colonel 11*th Pennsylvania Cavalry.*"

Major General Peck and Brigadier General R. S. Foster, both gave him high testimonials for acts of bravery and personal daring in the execution of orders under their immediate commands. Butts resigned on account of ill health; had contracted ague and fever in the low lands of Virginia. He commenced the practice of law in Norfolk. With his young and chivalrous spirit he saw what he knew was wrong. He represented it as a citizen to his Government. For that he was exiled.

GENERAL BUTLER'S MILITARY ADMINISTRATION IN THE FIELD.

Since General Butler has been so vigilant in trying to impress the public mind that the civil government was inefficient at Norfolk, it may not be amiss to advert to *his* administration of military affairs in the field in that vicinity. The first movement was to send about one hundred men to Smithfield, on the James river, in the face of the enemy, with no mode of retreat, and only to be supported by gunboats going up a creek that is little more than a quagmire at low tide. The result was the loss of the whole command, and the destruction of a gunboat, which got aground.

The next was General Wild's notable raid into North Carolina and Princess Anne county. I never want to see the history of that raid until the war is over. The taking of Miss White a prisoner is only one of the occurrences.

The next was the projected raid on Richmond, for the liberation of the Union prisoners. The failure was much regretted. It was attributed to the desertion of a Union soldier, who carried the news to Richmond, and gave them time to rally and defeat the project. And the public have been amused and satisfied with this story, and General Butler lauded to the heavens for the conception of the noble idea. He insulted the Navy by attributing to the officers unfaithfulness, and imprisoned a lady thirteen days, keeping her on bread and water, to force her to tell what naval officer had told her of the contemplated expedition to Richmond, when she knew nothing about it. Of all of this the public was duly notified through the press. But is it not strange how the soldier who deserted knew anything about the objects of the army, so as to give the information so long beforehand? It is said of General Harrison, when he commanded at Fort Meigs, in the winter of 1812, that there was a report of the approaching enemy, and some young man asked him what he was going to do, in case the enemy were at a certain point. The General replied that if he thought his shirt knew his thoughts, he would burn it. I heard this when I was very young, and it impressed me. I was impressed when I heard the story of the deserter. I asked the first four or five men I met from Norfolk if it was known there publicly before the expedition started that it was going. Every one of them replied that they knew it from six to ten days before it started. The troops that were going, the object, route, and all about it. It was told by his own officers. General Butler knew to whom he had confided his plans. Why did he not strike there for the person who revealed the secret? I think it very likely that the news of the raid was communicated from Norfolk to Richmond, and it was suggested in the letter, "publish that you got this news from a Union soldier who deserted." But it was known at Williamsburg, and talked of among the soldiers for at least six days before the expedition started. Yet censure is heaped on everybody, to keep observation from General Butler and his confidential advisers.

The last military exploit I heard of, was a raid into North Carolina and the capture of two lighter loads of corn and meal, with some contrabands, and the selling of the corn at public auction, and the proceeds of sale went into the *provost marshal's fund.*

With all the ridicule of General Butler, and the sneers of his *New Regime*, at the civil government of Norfolk and Portsmouth, it will stand out in bold relief as effective, when compared with General Butler's military operations in the field in that section.

The last I heard from the provost court, they were very desirous of trying a case of *habeas corpus* to determine the custody of two children, between a husband and wife who had separated.

WHAT BECOMES OF THE PROVOST MARSHAL'S FUND.

I might answer this question by repeating the question, what does become of it? Perhaps this is about as satisfactory an answer as the country will ever get.

It does not go into the Treasury of the United States, nor do I suppose it relieves it of any of its burdens. It is estimated by those who have pretty good opportunity of knowing, that there has been collected since General Butler went to Old Point last fall, from two to three hundred thousand dollars into this fund. There has been a system of excessive fines introduced for one supposed offense and another, varying from fifty to five thousand dollars. In addition to this mode, property, captured and confiscated, all goes into the *provost marshal's fund*, with tax on goods shipped into and out of the district, tax on oysters and dogs, clearances of vessels, &c., &c.

Some repairs are being made on the streets. This is done by convicts, soldiers and citizens in penitentiary uniform, with Government teams to do the hauling, superintended by a contractor. He may be paid for all that is done. Advertisements in the *New Regime*, and it is said there are about forty detectives there, all under pay, perhaps, to keep down the fund. But as to its disposition, all is conjecture. One thing is certain, there is great interest taken in enlarging the fund. One man got a permit to bring in three thousand dollars' worth of goods, and paid thirty dollars. His wife was taken ill, and remained sick for some time. He could not leave home, and when she got well he had to decline his enterprise. He called to get his money back, but was refused. Buck & Whitehurst got a permit last fall to bring in thirty thousand dollars' worth of some kind of goods, but the permit was delayed so long that the season passed for the sale of the article; they only brought in ten thousand dollars' worth. They called for their two hundred dollars paid on the permit they did not use, and were also prohibited from shipping anything more; but they could not get back their two hundred dollars. The Government would refund under such circumstances.

In this succinct statement I have only given a few cases. I don't know that they are the worst cases. An elaborate history might be written of the acts there, all interesting in detail, and tending to illustrate more fully the existence of systematic abuse of military power. I am informed that the same system prevails perhaps to a greater extent in North Carolina than in Virginia, because there is less restraint there. Civil government seems to check it a little—hence the anxiety to break it up, in order that they may have a clear field.

It is strange to me that such a system should have grown up whereby military commanders collect tens and hundreds of thousands of dollars into this post or provost marshal's fund which is held by men who give no bonds. None of it goes into the United States Treasury, but little of it to relieve the Treasury of its burdens, and much of it expended for objects in no way connected with the suppression of the rebellion. This, to my mind, is a subject which needs attention.

THE EFFECT OF ALL THIS ON THE PUBLIC MIND.

On going to Norfolk about the 20th of March last, I was humiliated. At Old Point and Norfolk, I met men, who, six months ago, stood erect and talked like freemen, who were proud of their country, and that they were American citizens. But now the hand of oppression is upon them, they look dejected and disheartened. When they spoke to me of their troubles, it was far from the presence of any one, and then in an undertone. When they came into my room to talk with me, they would look around the room to assure themselves that there was no spy concealed, and see that the doors were closely shut. The Union papers have been regretting that the Union cause for some time past has been on the decline in North Carolina. It is true. The wail of the oppressed there under General Butler's rule has gone out through the old North State and hushed the clamor of her liberty-loving people for the blessings of freedom they expected to enjoy under the old stars and stripes. And these oppressions now form the principal staple for the rebel

Governor Vance in his canvass for re-election, to persuade the people to be reconciled to Jeff. Davis's despotism.

In October last I felt hopeful and buoyant at the prospect of returning loyalty, and the disposition of the people to sustain the restored government. General Foster was in command of the department. I found him a gentleman and a soldier, earnest in his profession and desire to do right. General Barnes was placed in command of the two cities. He was from Massachusetts, an educated, earnest soldier, and all you would expect in a Massachusetts gentleman. Massachusetts, God bless her! I love her people. In Virginia's darkest day, in 1861, while the committee of safety was guiding, to a certain extent, the destiny of the loyal people of the State, the lightning of heaven brought us the happy dispatch from Governor Andrews that Massachusetts would let the loyal men of Virginia have two thousand muskets to be used in the defense of liberty in the State. A messenger was immediately dispatched for the arms. They came, and immediately on the reorganization of the State, I placed them in the hands of the men, where they did good service. The sending of the arms gave great moral strength to the Union cause and to Union hearts, and I say again, I love Massachusetts. It is an old adage, "that there are few mothers with many children but there are some black sheep among them." Massachusetts has hers, and I am after them. But I was speaking of General Barnes. He took great interest in the civil affairs of this section. General Lockwood was doing the same in Accomac and Northampton. The civil officers began to feel assured that they were going to be sustained, were taking courage, and civil affairs began to move off smoothly. But General Lockwood and General Barnes did not suit General Butler, and they were removed from his department. Before General Butler went there, the Union men were buoyant with the hope of seeing their section settled and repopulated by people from the North. They welcomed Northern men among them. But now dejection, despondency and bitterness is seen where hope then existed, and deep sectional hostility is beginning to manifest itself. Oh! it is a bitter, *bitter* contemplation, to see so glorious a cause as the Union cause thus stricken and wounded in the house of its friends. My heart is sick, *sick* at the contemplation. But there is consolation in knowing that the abuses only exist in this city and the district of Virginia and North Carolina, and that you, gentlemen, form a tribunal to whom we can appeal, which is too high and too pure to refuse adequate relief.

THE REMEDY.

I am asked is it too late to remedy the evil and restore the cause? I answer, no. The remedy is indicated by the inspired prophet in his declaration that "righteousness exalteth the nation, and sin is a reproach to any people." Then the remedy is in doing right. This is the easiest matter in the world. Sin is a reproach, that is, doing wrong, and it always brings trouble. Rebels will never be fully punished in this world. Many universalists have abandoned their favorite dogma of a universal heaven since this war commenced. They see plainly that there can be no adequate punishment on earth for those who have brought the calamities of this terrible war on the country. If fifty men in Virginia had done six years ago what fifty thousand have done in the last three years, they all would have been hung. But the Government thinks it not wise to undertake to kill everybody who has turned traitor. I think that is right. When Korah, Dathan, and Abiram, with the two hundred and fifty princes rebelled against Moses, the earth opened and they were swallowed up; a consuming flame came out and killed the two hundred and fifty princes, and the people who were led away by them fled to the side of Moses and were not hurt. Perhaps we have an example in this, that it is right to extend amnesty to all but the leaders in rebellion. It is certainly the prerogative of the Government to fix the terms of amnesty to rebels. If the Government had declared they should all be killed, and had killed as fast as we got to them, it would be difficult to prove that it was not a just act. Slavery was the root of the rebellion. Perhaps its abolishment, with confiscation, will be punishishment enough. But the President, for wise purposes, determined that all who would return to allegiance, from the grade of colonel and under, and take the oath he prescribed, *should be pardoned and restored to all their rights of property*, unless it had been sold under the laws punishing traitors. But if confiscations had commenced and not prosecuted to sale, the proceedings are to be dismissed upon the rebels taking the oath. The fullest and amplest protection is offered. General Butler has ordered all in his military district to take the oath with the solemn pledge of protection; the nation is bound to guarantee it. It is right to guarantee it after it is made. The Government, through the President, has prescribed the terms by which the rebel is to be protected. He conforms to the requisition, the terms must be kept on our part. A great Government like the United States cannot afford to do *wrong.* Now, it is *right* to redress all the wrongs General Butler has committed in his district as far as possible. It is *right* to return the gas works to the proper owners, with a fair charge for the repairs, and an account for the profits and especially to return the thirteen hundred dollars which were in the safe. It is *right* to return to Mrs. Tatem her silver cake baskets; to return to the proper owners the silver taken from the house of Mr. Bilisolly, and also the wine and brandy taken from his house, and if it cannot be returned to punish those who have put it out of the power of the Government to do *right.* It is *right* to return to Daniels & Zantzinger the fifteen thousand dollars taken from them, and to reimburse Hodgins for violently turning him out of his house, and those who occupy the house should pay the money; and to require the speculators to reimburse the farmers whose land they have stripped of timber, if these farmers have taken the oath and have not violated it. Williams and all the other parties that have been turned out of their houses should have their property restored to them, where they have taken the oath and not violated it. This done, and there is no fair man living but will say it is *right* that it should be done; this would be that kind of righteousness which exalteth a nation. The news of its being ordered would thrill the hearts of the Union men in rebeldom. It would be grateful to every loyal heart in the nation, and would create a little jubilee in those desponding hearts in this section. Loyalty would prevail, and blessings would be poured out of grateful hearts upon the Government, where secret curses and imprecations are now being indulged in; and as General Grant goes south this spring, hundreds of thousands will flock around his banner and kiss the old flag, conscious that no wrong will be suffered where it floats. It will disarm hundreds of thousands of their stubbornness, and save the lives of thousands of Union soldiers. I am satisfied that these oppressions have done more to unite the rebels in the south and retard Union sentiment there, though confined to a narrow compass as they are, than any thing that has occurred since the rebellion has commenced, and if not corrected their warning voice will go into the south, and General Grant as he goes forward this summer, with his noble comrades, will have a hard road to travel.

The natural condition of men is under civil government. The military is an organized artificial force to aid the civil law to assert its power when resisted by force. It is *right* that the civil discharge all the duties assigned it by society; if resisted, the military removes the resistance; when that is done it has performed its function. Whenever it attempts to discharge civil duties it is *wrong*, and begets discord. It is *right* for the officers to attend to the duties assigned them by the rules of war; to drill and discipline the soldier; to prepare him for effective duty; to look after his health, and, as far as possible, to preserve his morals; to lead him in battle, and in all things to set him a good example. War is expensive, both in money and life, hence it should be short. I think there can be no controversy about these propositions being right in theory; and their practicable application is this. If the military will drive all the rebel army out of the State I will reorganize every county in the State in less than six months, with loyal officers to execute the civil laws. If they will remove all the soldiers from the limits of the city of Alexandria, Norfolk and Portsmouth, except what may be necessary to guard the public stores, and pick up straggling soldiers that come into the cities, I will ensure the good government of all three of the cities through the civil government, and save the Federal Government at least thirty thousand dollars per annum by way of pay to military brigadiers and their staffs, and superfluous bands of music, for which the civil government will not charge one cent. I submit, in all earnestness, that the city of Norfolk, for instance, with fifteen hundred women congregated there "who are no better than they ought to be," is not the place for soldiers or officers, who are expected to do efficient work in the field. In the city is not the place for the officer or soldier to defend the city. Philadelphia and Washington are defended and protected by the Army of the Potomac. Norfolk and Alexandria should be protected by the army outside of the cities, and there is no sort of military necessity for a military governor being in either city—a battalion with a field officer as commandant of the post is all that is necessary.

It will greatly relieve the complication of matters at Norfolk to open the port, and appoint an honest collector. He could attend to the business with half the cost to the Government and much more benefit to all concerned. This would greatly diminish the stock of goods kept on hand in those cities. This must be evident to any person who has observed the practical workings of the present system. A merchant now applies at Norfolk for a permit to ship goods into the city; he gets it signed there; he then sends it to Washington for approval; it is then sent to the custom house at Baltimore. This is done in a week; sometimes two or three weeks transpire; hence, a merchant to avoid trouble of permit, gets large supplies; and lest he should run out, replenishes soon; keeping on hand a large surplus; but open the ports, dispense with the permits, and he can send to Baltimore and get a return in 48 hours at furthest. Their cargoes with their invoices would be subject to inspection by custom house officers. The same regulations would still have to be kept up as to blockade runners. But I would dispense with much of that force by hanging or shooting all the blockade runners caught. These rascals have no claim upon their lives when they put the country to millions of expense to watch them, besides a large number of soldiers exposed to premature disease. In all such cases, when fairly detected, they should be hung. I think they are worse than spies. They combine the spy and the thief.

The loyal people of Norfolk and Portsmouth paid nearly $25,000 of internal revenue last year; I do not know how much this. Many of them, however, have paid large amounts of internal revenue for licenses that have not been permitted to use them; others commenced using and were closed up by the caprice of military commanders, and to make way for those who are in the same trade as monopolists. This is a reproach.

I submit these suggestions with great deference. But the subjects I have embraced are so deeply interesting to the people I represent, that did I not call them to your attention I should be grossly criminal.

I have been just as close to this war, ever since it commenced, as I could without much danger of being hurt, and have observed as closely as I could all the time. I think I understand the subject about which I am writing, and I am satisfied that if the military rule had been practiced in West Virginia as it was in Alexandria for the last eighteen months, and in Norfolk for the last five months, that instead of the vast majority of loyal Union men that are there now sustaining the Government with men and money, and with happiness and prosperity around them, there would have been a vast majority of copperheads and secessionists, and civil government could not have been sustained. Regiments that now fill the Union army would have been in the secession army. I mean precisely what I say.

The question has been asked me, I am satisfied, a thousand times, "Do the President and Congress know of the oppression practiced on us?" The people say, "We have great confidence in the President's honesty and the purity of Congress, and they will redress our wrongs." . I have an abiding confidence, gentlemen, in your justice.

I was born in Virginia. I desire to live in Virginia when this rebellion is subdued. I hope to see the old flag shortly unfurled in every county in the State, and the people acknowledging its majesty, and acknowledging with uplifted hands, the Constitution it represents to be the supreme law of the land. I never expect to have the *love* and *sympathy* of the rebels; but by the grace of God, by doing *right*, I intend to command their respect. My ardent desire and sincere prayer is, that this rebellion may be speedily crushed, that freedom may be enjoyed, not only in the State, but in all the broad limits of the nation, and that when the impartial historian comes to make up the record, he may be able truthfully to publish, that in accomplishing this great result the Government never sanctioned a *wrong* that was done to any man, however humble.

majority of Republicans and secessionists, and civil government could not have been sustained." Regiments that now fill the Union army would have been [illegible] [illegible]. I mean precisely what I say.

The question has been asked me [illegible] [illegible] Does the President and Congress [illegible] [illegible] [illegible] [illegible]. The people [illegible] [illegible] [illegible] the honesty and [illegible] of [illegible] [illegible] with [illegible] [illegible] [illegible] gentlemen, [illegible] justice.

I [illegible] [illegible] I desire to [illegible] Virginia [illegible] [illegible] [illegible]. I hope to see the old [illegible] [illegible] [illegible] the [illegible] [illegible] [illegible] [illegible] [illegible] [illegible] [illegible] [illegible] and [illegible]. I [illegible] to have the [illegible] [illegible] the [illegible] of God, [illegible].

APPENDIX.

The following letter from General Butler appeared in the *New Regime*, his own organ, published in Norfolk, and has been copied into some of the papers in the country. Lest it may mislead the public, I propose to expose the statements therein made. I publish the letter in full:

HEADQUARTERS 18TH ARMY CORPS,
DEPARTMENT OF VA. AND N. C.,
FORTRESS MONROE, *May* 4, 1864.

SIR: I have received your note saying that you are assessing for State licenses for 1864, and further that "the regulations giving the privilege of bringing spirituous liquors into the city to a few persons only is giving dissatisfaction to many persons, and will reduce the number of licenses, and consequently the revenues from this source."

You then further give me your opinion that restricting the sale of liquors to a few persons will not reduce the consumption, and that you think that all merchants of good standing should have the privilege, and that you are satisfied that I did not make the regulation in the interest of the few.

I have given licenses to twelve persons to sell liquor in Norfolk, they keeping accurate books to whom they sell, and they are held responsible for the purposes to which it goes, to the extent of their licenses. If the license is a valuable thing to them, that makes a check upon their actions. I was informed before the order issued, that the *soi disant* Governor of Virginia, Peirpoint, had complained that the non-granting of liquor licenses in Alexandria by Gen. Slough had nearly bankrupted the Treasury of Virginia. I think a State which cannot exist without deriving its principle revenue from the unrestricted sale of poisonous liquors to its inhabitants, had better get itself out of existence.

If my regulations in this regard should have that effect upon such a State as I have described, it would be a source of congratulation. Twelve (12) persons selling liquor at retail, and all respectable hotels selling it to their guests, would seem to be enough, in a city of ten thousand whites and five thousand blacks, to engender pauperism and crime, and prevent monopoly, and as you and I agree that the less sold the better, the more restriction thrown around the sale the less will be sold, is the universal law of trade.

I have the personal acquaintance, and prior to the granting of their licences have never spoken to or seen but two of the twelve persons to whom this permit was given. After the twelve were filled up, one of my warmest and oldest personal friends in trade in Norfolk, I was obliged to refuse, because I had fixed the number at twelve. Because of this, I have been abused by the supposed Governor of the State of Virginia, in a scurrilous pamphlet, which is the only aid I have received from him since taking charge of this Department, towards suppressing the rebellion or in governing a disarranged community.

I have done what I believe to be right in this regard, and neither the opinions of the assessor—for whom I entertain a high respect—nor the abuse of the Governor will be very likely to move me from my position.

I have the honor to be, very respectfully, your obedient servant,

BENJ. F. BUTLER.

To JOHN F. DUNN, Assessor, 4th District of Virginia, Norfolk, Va.

I desire to call particular attention to the first paragraph. He commenced by saying "I have received your note saying that you are collecting State license for 1864, and further that," &c.

Observe the residue of the paragraph is in quotation marks. No man can read this letter without coming to the

5 P

conclusion that Mr. Dunn is the assessor of State revenue. When the fact is he has nothing to do with State revenue, but is the assessor of United States internal revenue for the fourth district of Virginia.

He further says: "I have given licenses to twelve persons to sell liquor in Norfolk. * * * Twelve persons selling at retail, and all respectable hotel keepers selling to their guests," &c.

This is a singular statement; when it is known that hotel keepers and restaurant keepers both sell to their guests to be drank where sold, and also retail it to be carried away in bottles. There must be more than twelve who sell by retail, according to the General's own statement. Yet "after the twelve were filled up he *denied his old personal friend a license,*" because he had fixed the number at twelve. This needs explanation. The facts are these: when General Butler wrote this letter on the 4th of May and up to the 14th of May, and up to this date, there were only eight (8) persons or firms permitted by General Butler to *bring* liquors into the city of Norfolk, and there were *thirty-six* (36) hotel and restaurant keepers selling by retail, but not one of these thirty-six were permitted to buy any of their liquors in Baltimore, or any other city, outside of the city of Norfolk but *the thirty-six* had to buy of these eight monopolists at extortionate prices—never at less than one hundred and frequently at two hundred per cent. profit on the cost at Baltimore or New York. Of these favored monopolists four came from Massachusetts, after General Butler came there, three from New York, and one from Pennsylvania. This is a somewhat singular selection if it happened by chance. What sensible man in the United States does not understand this whole transaction in regard to the monopoly? If it is to restrain the use why not limit them to small profits—*that was not in the license.*

The General thinks these are enough "*to engender pauperism and crime*" in a population of fifteen thousand. I think so too, and neither advised or counseled it, and if anybody is responsible for it, it is the veritable General Butler. There was but one firm, Zantzinger & Co., that were selling in very moderate quantities, under strict military orders, when he went there. He closed them up to make way for the monopolists, appropriating fifteen thousand dollars of their money to the *provost marshal's fund*, when, if it were right to take it, it should have gone into the Treasury of the

United States, according to the act of Congress in such case made and provided.

He "was informed," * * * "that the *soi disant* Governor of Virginia, Peirpoint, had complained that the non-granting of liquor licenses in Alexandria by General Slough had nearly bankrupted the treasury of Virginia."

The committee of Congress on the Conduct of the War in a report made public, state "That the State authorities urged that if they were deprived of the revenue which might be derived from licensing the traffic in liquor, the salaries of the State officers and other expenses could not be paid." Both General Butler and the committee have been imposed on in regard to this statement. I know its origin, and it has no more foundation than if they had stated that the salary of the President and members of Congress could not be paid unless the traffic in liquor was licensed in Virginia. Peirpoint and the State authorities never urged any such thing. The State treasury has not had in it, at any time for the last eight months, less than fifty thousand dollars.

"Because of this," says the General, "I have been abused by the supposed Governor of Virginia in a scurrilous pamphlet." This is one of Butler's sharp "turns," as his admirers would term it; but it is a piece of much that proceeds from him—has more of the low cunning than anything else. He seeks to make the impression that it was because of an honest effort on his part to restrict the sale of liquors in Norfolk, that I had "abused" him in a "scurrilous" pamphlet. This is not the first time since this war commenced that I have seen the maladministration of military officers sought to be covered up by the sweeping charge that the general was only trying to restrict the sale of liquor. When that object is honestly sought after it is a virtue. I desire now to say, once for all, in regard to the traffic in liquor, in my opinion it is the worst evil in the United States Army, and if any general having authority, will suppress its use in Virginia, I will be the last man to object; but where I see its general sale attempted to be suppressed, and at the same time a number of men permitted to carry on the business through favoritism for purposes of speculation and monopoly, and the use of the evil is not diminished thereby, I shall continue to denounce the practice as odious, demoralizing to the citizen and soldier. However pure the general may be who practices it, the belief will exist in the community and among the soldiers that he is a party in some way to the speculation; and it has the worst effect on the public mind, weakening respect for public authority. But General Butler knew when he penned that sentence that I had not said one word in my pamphlet about the restriction of the sale of liquors where the object was to diminish the amount used; but it was the *monopoly to strangers*, withholding all privileges from citizens, which was odious, and I denounced it. But that was only a single charge among many abuses of military power that I made public. If a statement of facts, which are abuses of military power constitute *abuse* and *scurrility*, then I am liable to the charge. The General sent the silver home as soon as he received my pamphlet, but the wine and brandy were retained. This is an acknowledgment of the justice of my charge.

"This," says he, "is the only aid I have received from him since taking charge of this department towards suppressing the rebellion or in governing this disarranged community."

I kindly proffered my aid and counsel to General Butler to assist in governing that "disarranged community;" but instead of taking counsel from me, he preferred calling in Tazwell Taylor to his counsel, the most noted secessionist in Norfolk, to counsel how he might overthrow the civil government. Taylor had taken a prominent part in overthrowing the United States Government in a large part of Virginia. He was deemed fit counsel for General Butler, who desired to overthrow the restored government of the State. I prescribed to myself a rule in the outset of this rebellion not to call into my confidence and counsel rebels against my Government, who were seeking its overthrow, nor to consult with generals who did; and when I found General Butler had called Tazwell Taylor to his counsel I resolved to not offer him mine, and I now inform him that he has done more to *disarrange* that community than any man living except Jeff. Davis and his followers.

"I have done what I believe to be right in this regard," says the General, "and neither the opinion of the assessor nor the abuse of the Governor will be very likely to move me from my position." I presume neither will be likely to move him from his position; but there is a very prevalent opinion that his blunders, if nothing else, in the command of his military department, will be very likely to "move" him from his "position."

F. H. PEIRPOINT.

www.ingramcontent.com/pod-product-compliance
Lightning Source LLC
Chambersburg PA
CBHW021634270326
41931CB00008B/1021
* 9 7 8 3 3 3 7 2 3 4 2 5 6 *